Contents

Acknowledgements

The authors and publishers acknowledge the following sources of photographs

p. 17 Tao Images/Robert Harding; p. 20 Richard Wong/Alamy; p. 22 Edward Bock/Corbis; p. 37 Greg Balfour Evans/Alamy; p. 40 Image Source/Corbis; p. 42 Lockwood_Dattatri/ naturepl.com; p. 57 PCN Photography/Alamy; p. 60 Antographer/Alamy; p. 62 Gavin Hellier/ Alamy; p. 77 amana images inc./Alamy; p. 80 AlamyCelebrity/Alamy; p. 82 Design Pics/ Ben Welsh/Getty Images

Picture research by Joanne Robinson

Book design by Peter Ducker MSTD

Cover design by David Lawton

The CD which accompanies this book was recorded at dsound, London.

A guide to Cambridge English: Key

Cambridge English: Key, also known as the *Key English Test (KET)*, is part of a comprehensive range of exams developed by University of Cambridge ESOL Examinations (Cambridge ESOL). Cambridge English exams have similar characteristics but are designed for different purposes and different levels of English language ability. *Cambridge English: Key* is at Level A2 (Waystage) of the Council of Europe's Common European Framework of Reference for Languages (CEFR). It has also been accredited in the UK as an Entry Level 2 ESOL certificate in the UK's National Qualifications Framework.

Examination	Council of Europe Framework Level	UK National Qualifications Framework Level
Cambridge English: Proficiency *Certificate of Proficiency in English (CPE)*	C2	3
Cambridge English: Advanced *Certificate in Advanced English (CAE)*	C1	2
Cambridge English: First *First Certificate in English (FCE)*	B2	1
Cambridge English: Preliminary *Preliminary English Test (PET)*	B1	Entry 3
Cambridge English: Key *Key English Test (KET)*	A2	Entry 2

Cambridge English: Key is accepted by employers, further education and government departments for business, study and immigration purposes. It is also useful preparation for higher level exams, such as *Cambridge English: Preliminary* and *Cambridge English: First*.

Cambridge English: Key is a great first step in English. Preparing for the exam will build your confidence in dealing with everyday written and spoken English at a basic level, for example expressing and understanding simple opinions; filling in forms; and writing short, simple letters.

Cambridge English: Key is also available in a version with exam content and topics specifically targeted at the interests and experience of school-aged learners. *Cambridge English: Key for Schools*, also known as the *Key English Test (KET) for Schools*, follows exactly the same format and level and leads to the same certificate as *Cambridge English: Key*.

Topics

These are the topics used in the *Cambridge English: Key* exam:

Clothes	People	Shopping
Daily life	Personal feelings, opinions	Social interaction
Entertainment and media	and experiences	The natural world
Food and drink	Personal identification	Transport
Health, medicine and exercise	Places and buildings	Travel and holidays
Hobbies and leisure	School and study	Weather
House and home	Services	Work and jobs
Language		

Overview of the exam

Paper	Name	Timing	Content	Test focus
Paper 1	Reading/ Writing	1 hour 10 minutes	Nine parts: Five parts (Parts 1–5) test a range of reading skills with a variety of texts, ranging from very short notices to longer continuous texts. Parts 6–9 concentrate on testing basic writing skills.	Assessment of candidates' ability to understand the meaning of written English at word, phrase, sentence, paragraph and whole text level. Assessment of candidates' ability to produce simple written English, ranging from one-word answers to a short piece of continuous text.
Paper 2	Listening	30 minutes (including 8 minutes transfer time)	Five parts, ranging from short exchanges to longer dialogues and monologues.	Assessment of candidates' ability to understand dialogues and monologues in both informal and neutral settings on a range of everyday topics.
Paper 3	Speaking	8–10 minutes per pair of candidates	Two parts: In Part 1, candidates interact with an examiner. In Part 2, they interact with another candidate.	Assessment of candidates' ability to answer and ask questions about themselves and about factual, non-personal information.

Paper 1 Reading and Writing

Paper format

The Reading section contains five parts. The Writing section contains four parts.

Number of questions

There is a total of 56 questions: 35 in Reading and 21 in Writing.

Sources

Authentic and adapted-authentic real-world notices, newspaper and magazine articles, simplified encyclopaedia entries.

Answering

Candidates indicate answers either by shading lozenges (Reading) or by writing answers (Writing) on an answer sheet.

Timing

1 hour 10 minutes.

Marks

Each item carries one mark, except for question 56 (Part 9), which is marked out of 5. This gives a total of 60 marks, which is weighted to a final mark out of 50. This represents 50% of the total marks for the whole examination.

Preparing for the Reading section

To prepare for the Reading section, you should read the type of English used in everyday life; for example, short newspaper and magazine articles, advertisements, tourist brochures, instructions and recipes, etc. It is also a good idea to practise reading short communicative messages, including notes, emails and cards. Remember, you won't always need to understand every word to be able to do a task in the exam.

Before the exam, think about the time you need to do each part and check you know how to record your answers on the answer sheet (see page 148).

Part	Task type and format	Task focus	Number of questions
1	Matching. Matching five prompt sentences to eight notices, plus an example.	Gist understanding of real-world notices. Reading for main message.	5
2	Three-option multiple choice. Five sentences (plus an integrated example) with connecting link of topic or storyline.	Reading and identifying appropriate vocabulary.	5

3	Three-option multiple choice. Five discrete three-option multiple-choice items (plus an example) focusing on verbal exchange patterns. **AND** Matching. Five matching items (plus an example) in a continuous dialogue, selecting from eight possible responses.	Functional language. Reading and identifying the appropriate response.	10
4	Right/Wrong/Doesn't say **OR** Three-option multiple choice. One long text or three short texts adapted from authentic newspaper or magazine articles. Seven three-option multiple-choice items or Right/Wrong/Doesn't say items, plus an example.	Reading for detailed understanding and main idea(s).	7
5	Multiple-choice cloze. A text adapted from an original source, for example an encyclopaedia entry, newspaper or magazine article. Eight three-option multiple-choice items, plus an integrated example.	Reading and identifying appropriate structural words (auxiliary verbs, modal verbs, determiners, pronouns, prepositions, conjunctions, etc.).	8

Preparing for the Writing section

To prepare for the Writing section, you should take the opportunity to write short messages in real-life situations, for example to your teacher or other students. These can include invitations, arrangements for meetings, apologies for missing a class, or notices about lost property. They can be handwritten or sent as email.

Before the exam, think about the time you need to do each part and check you know how to record your answers on the answer sheet (see page 149).

Part	Task type and format	Task focus	Number of questions
6	Word completion. Five dictionary definition type sentences (plus an example). Five words to identify and spell.	Reading and identifying appropriate vocabulary, and spelling.	5
7	Open cloze. Text type that candidates can be expected to write, for example a short letter or email. Ten spaces to fill with one word which must be spelled correctly, (plus an integrated example).	Reading and identifying appropriate words, with a focus on structure and/or vocabulary.	10
8	Information transfer. Two short authentic texts (emails, adverts, etc.) to prompt completion of another text (form, note, etc.). Five spaces to fill with one or more words or numbers (plus an integrated example).	Reading and writing appropriate words or numbers, with a focus on content and accuracy.	5
9	Guided writing. Either a short input text or a rubric to prompt a written response. Three messages to communicate in writing.	Writing a short message, note, email or postcard of 25–35 words.	1

Part 6

This part is about vocabulary. You have to produce words and spell them correctly. The words will all be linked to the same topic, for example jobs or food. You have to read a definition for each one and complete the word. The first letter of each word is given to help you.

Part 7

This part is about grammar and vocabulary. You have to complete a short, gapped text of the type you could be expected to write, such as a note, email or short letter. You must spell all the missing words correctly.

Part 8

This part tests both reading and writing. You have to use the information in two short texts (for example a note, email or advertisement) to complete a document such as a form, notice or diary entry. You will need to understand the vocabulary used on forms, for example *name*, *cost* and *time*. You will need to write only words or phrases in your answers, but you must spell them correctly.

Part 9

You have to write a short message (25–35 words). You are told who you are writing to and why, and you must include three pieces of information. To gain top marks, all three parts of the message must be included in your answer, so it is important to read the question carefully and plan what you are going to write. Before the exam, practise writing answers of the correct length. You will lose marks for writing fewer than 25 words, and it is not a good idea to write answers that are too long.

Mark Scheme for Part 9

There are five marks for Part 9. Minor grammatical and spelling mistakes are acceptable, but to get five marks you must write a clear message and include all three pieces of information.

Mark	Criteria	
5	All three parts of the message clearly communicated.	
	Only minor spelling errors or occasional grammatical errors.	
4	All three parts of the message communicated.	
	Some non-impeding errors in spelling and grammar or some awkwardness of expression.	
3	All three parts of the message attempted.	Two parts of the message clearly communicated.
	Expression requires interpretation by the reader and contains impeding errors in spelling and grammar.	Only minor spelling errors or occasional grammatical errors.
2	Only two parts of the message communicated.	
	Some errors in spelling and grammar.	
	The errors in expression may require patience and interpretation by the reader and impede communication.	
1	Only one part of the message communicated.	
0	Question unattempted, or totally incomprehensible response.	

Paper 2   Listening

Paper format

This paper contains five parts.

Number of questions

25

Task types

Matching, multiple choice, gap-fill.

Sources

All texts are based on authentic situations, and each part is heard twice.

Answering

Candidates indicate answers either by shading lozenges (Parts 1–3) or by writing answers (Parts 4 and 5) on an answer sheet.

Timing

About 30 minutes, including 8 minutes to transfer answers.

Marks

Each item carries one mark. This gives a total of 25 marks, which represents 25% of the total marks for the examination.

Preparing for the Listening test

The best preparation for the Listening test is to listen to authentic spoken English for your level. Apart from in class, other sources of English include films, TV, DVDs, songs, the internet, English clubs, and other speakers of English such as tourists, guides, friends and family.

You will hear the instructions for each task on the recording and see them on the exam paper. There are pauses in the recording to give you time to look at the questions and to write your answers. You should write your answers on the exam paper as you listen. You will have eight minutes at the end of the test to transfer your answers to the answer sheet (see page 150). Make sure you know how to do this and that you check your answers carefully.

Part	Task type and format	Task focus	Number of questions
1	Three-option multiple choice. Short, neutral or informal dialogues. Five discrete three-option multiple-choice items with pictures (plus an example).	Listening to identify key information (times, prices, days of week, numbers, etc.).	5
2	Matching. Longer informal dialogue. Five items (plus an integrated example) and eight options.	Listening to identify key information.	5
3	Three-option multiple choice. Longer informal or neutral dialogue. Five three-option multiple-choice items (plus an integrated example).	Taking the role of one of the speakers and listening to identify key information.	5
4	Gap-fill. Longer neutral or informal dialogue. Five gaps to fill with one or more words or numbers (plus an integrated example). Recognisable spelling is accepted, except with very high-frequency words (e.g. *bus*, *red*) or if spelling is dictated.	Listening and writing down information (including spelling of names, places, etc. as dictated on recording).	5
5	Gap-fill. Longer neutral or informal monologue. Five gaps to fill with one or more words or numbers (plus an integrated example). Recognisable spelling is accepted, except with very high-frequency words (e.g. *bus*, *red*) or if spelling is dictated.	Listening and writing down information (including spelling of names, places, etc. as dictated on recording).	5

Paper 3 Speaking

Paper format

The paper contains two parts. The standard format for Paper 3 is two candidates and two examiners. One examiner acts only as an assessor and does not join in the conversation. The other examiner is called the interlocutor and manages the interaction by asking questions and setting up the tasks (see Paper 3 frames on pages 104–115).

Task types

Short exchanges with the interlocutor and an interactive task involving both candidates.

Timing

8–10 minutes per pair of candidates.

Marks

Candidates are assessed on their performance throughout the test. There are a total of 25 marks, making 25% of the total score for the whole examination.

Preparing for the Speaking test

Take every opportunity to practise your English with as many people as possible. Asking and answering questions in simple role plays provides useful practice. These role plays should focus on everyday language and situations, and involve questions about daily activities and familiar experiences. It is also a good idea to practise exchanging information in role plays about things such as the costs and opening times of, for example, a local sports centre.

Part	Task type and format	Task focus	Timing
1	Each candidate interacts with the interlocutor. The interlocutor asks the candidates questions. The interlocutor follows an interlocutor frame to guide the conversation, ensure standardisation, and control the level of input.	Language normally associated with meeting people for the first time, giving information of a factual, personal kind. Bio-data type questions to respond to.	5–6 minutes
2	Candidates interact with each other. The interlocutor sets up the activity using a standardised rubric. Candidates ask and answer questions using prompt material.	Factual information of a non-personal kind related to daily life.	3–4 minutes

Assessment

Throughout the Speaking test the examiners listen to what you say and give you marks for how well you speak English, so you must try to speak about the tasks and answer the examiner's and your partner's questions.

The two examiners mark different aspects of your speaking. One of the examiners (the assessor) will give marks on the following:

Grammar and Vocabulary

This refers to the range of language you use and also how accurately you use grammar and vocabulary.

Pronunciation

This refers to how easy it is to understand what you say. You should be able to say words and sentences that are easy to understand.

Interactive Communication

This refers to how well you can talk about a task, and to your partner and the examiner, and whether you can ask for repetition or clarification if needed.

Band	Grammar and Vocabulary	Pronunciation	Interactive Communication
5	• Shows a good degree of control of simple grammatical forms. • Uses a range of appropriate vocabulary when talking about everyday situations.	• Is mostly intelligible, and has some control of phonological features at both utterance and word levels.	• Maintains simple exchanges. • Requires very little prompting and support.
4	*Performance shares features of Bands 3 and 5.*		
3	• Shows sufficient control of simple grammatical forms. • Uses appropriate vocabulary to talk about everyday situations.	• Is mostly intelligible, despite limited control of phonological features.	• Maintains simple exchanges, despite some difficulty. • Requires prompting and support.
2	*Performance shares features of Bands 1 and 3.*		
1	• Shows only limited control of a few grammatical forms. • Uses a vocabulary of isolated words and phrases.	• Has very limited control of phonological features and is often unintelligible.	• Has considerable difficulty maintaining simple exchanges. • Requires additional prompting and support.
0	*Performance below Band 1.*		

The examiner asking the questions (the interlocutor) gives marks for how well you do overall, using a Global Achievement scale.

Band	Global Achievement
5	• Handles communication in everyday situations, despite hesitation. • Constructs longer utterances but is not able to use complex language except in well-rehearsed utterances.
4	*Performance shares features of Bands 3 and 5.*
3	• Conveys basic meaning in very familiar everyday situations. • Produces utterances which tend to be very short – words or phrases – with frequent hesitation and pauses.
2	*Performance shares features of Bands 1 and 3.*
1	• Has difficulty conveying basic meaning even in very familiar everyday situations. • Responses are limited to short phrases or isolated words with frequent hesitation and pauses.
0	*Performance below Band 1.*

Further information

The information in this practice book is designed to give an overview of *Cambridge English: Key*. For a full description of all the *Cambridge English* exams, including information about task types, testing focus and preparation, please see the relevant handbooks which can be obtained from Cambridge ESOL at the address below or from the website: www.CambridgeESOL.org.

University of Cambridge
ESOL Examinations
1 Hills Road
Cambridge
CB1 2EU
United Kingdom

Telephone: +44 1223 553355
Fax: +44 1223 460278
Email: ESOLHelpdesk@Cambridgeassessment.org.uk

Test 1

PAPER 1   READING AND WRITING (1 hour 10 minutes)

PART 1

QUESTIONS 1–5

Which notice (A–H) says this (1–5)?
For questions 1–5, mark the correct letter A–H on your answer sheet.

Example:

0   You can buy photographs in this shop that
were taken by someone who lives nearby.

Answer:

0	A	B	C	D	E	F	G	H
	☐	☐	☐	☐	■	☐	☐	☐

---

1   You can learn how to paint here.

A
> Passport photographs
> are ready in 5 minutes

2   If you go shopping here this week, you'll
pay much less than usual.

B
> Monica's art class will
> be in room 31 today

C
> City Museum
> Talk on 16th-century artists
> Wednesday, 6.30 pm   £2

3   This place is not open every day.

D
> The Art Centre library is
> now closed on Fridays

4   You won't have to wait long before you
get your pictures.

E
> Winton Stores
> Postcards by our village
> photographer on sale inside

F
> Homestore
> all paint half-price – for one month only

5   Someone has just painted a door in this
building.

G
> Wet Paint!
> Please use other entrance

H
> Burley Art Club
> Sale of paintings starts Monday

PART 2

QUESTIONS 6–10

Read the sentences about camping.
Choose the best word (A, B or C) for each space.
For questions 6–10, mark A, B or C on your answer sheet.

Example:

0   A lot of families prefer to .... on a campsite because it is cheaper than a hotel.

   A   keep   **B**   stay   **C**   travel   *Answer:*

0	A	B	C
	☐	■	☐

---

6   For some campsites, you have to phone and .... before you go.

   A   book   **B**   take   **C**   spend

7   Some people play loud music on campsites so it can be very ....

   A   angry   **B**   busy   **C**   noisy

8   One of the nicest things about camping is .... breakfast outside.

   A   doing   **B**   having   **C**   putting

9   It is better to use plastic cups and plates for camping because they don't .... easily.

   A   break   **B**   hurt   **C**   fail

10   One problem with camping is making .... insects don't get into the tent.

   A   careful   **B**   clear   **C**   sure

PART 3

QUESTIONS 11–15

Complete the five conversations.
For questions 11–15, mark A, B or C on your answer sheet.

Example:

0 Where do you come from?

A New York.

B School.

C Home.

Answer: **0** A B C ■ ☐ ☐

---

11 Is it a good film?

A That's right.

B It's OK.

C I don't agree.

12 I'm going to Tom's party tonight.

A Can I go too?

B Let's go.

C Was it good?

13 When did you lose your watch?

A Once a week.

B For six days.

C A month ago.

14 Sorry, I don't understand you.

A Let me explain.

B I don't know.

C What does it mean?

15 Shall we ask Paul to come with us?

A I believe it.

B I'm sure.

C If you like.

QUESTIONS 16–20

Complete the telephone conversation between two friends.
What does Jennifer say to Lily?
For questions 16–20, mark the correct letter A–H on your answer sheet.

Example:

Lily:	Hi Jennifer, it will be lovely to see you on Friday.
Jennifer:	0 ....**B**..............

Answer:

0	A B C D E F G H
	☐ ■ ☐ ☐ ☐ ☐ ☐ ☐

Lily:	What time is your train?		**A**	I have to go home at 6 o'clock.
Jennifer:	**16**		**B**	Yes, I haven't seen you for so long.
Lily:	OK. I'll meet you. Would you like to go out that evening?			
Jennifer:	**17**		**C**	I've heard it's really big.
Lily:	If you want to. Then on Saturday we can go to the new shopping centre.		**D**	Is he still living in the same house?
Jennifer:	**18**		**E**	It should arrive early afternoon.
Lily:	And in the evening we can go to Oliver's party.		**F**	How long will we stay with him there?
Jennifer:	**19**		**G**	I think I'll be tired. Shall we just stay at home?
Lily:	Oh anything. It doesn't matter.			
Jennifer:	**20**		**H**	Great! What should I bring to wear?
Lily:	Yes. It's a good place for a party. See you Friday, then.			

PART 4

QUESTIONS 21–27

Read the article about a man who swam across New Zealand's Cook Strait.
Are sentences 21–27 'Right' (A) or 'Wrong' (B)?
If there is not enough information to answer 'Right' (A) or 'Wrong' (B), choose
'Doesn't say' (C).
For questions 21–27, mark A, B or C on your answer sheet.

David swims the Cook Strait

David Johnson has loved swimming all his life. When he was 27, he swam in a race near his home in the USA. The sea was very cold and David started to feel unwell. He was taken to hospital but he soon got better and started swimming again. In 1983, he became the first person to swim from Santa Cruz Island to the Californian coast.

In January 2004, at the age of 52, David crossed New Zealand's Cook Strait in 9 hours and 38 minutes. The oldest swimmer before David was only 42 years old. David spent over a year getting ready to swim the Strait. Then, he and his wife flew to New Zealand so that David could practise for a few weeks there. But, only days after they arrived, the weather improved so David decided to start his swim. He did it with the help of a team. 'They were great,' David said. 'They were in a boat next to me all the time! After a few hours, I thought about stopping but I didn't and went on swimming.'

Afterwards, David and his wife travelled around New Zealand before returning to the USA.

Example:

0   David Johnson has always enjoyed swimming.

A   Right   **B**   Wrong   **C**   Doesn't say   *Answer:*

---

21   David Johnson had problems during a swimming competition in the USA.

A   Right   **B**   Wrong   **C**   Doesn't say

22   After 1983, many people swam between Santa Cruz Island and the Californian coast.

A   Right   **B**   Wrong   **C**   Doesn't say

23   In January 2004, David was the first person of his age to swim across the Cook Strait.

A   Right   **B**   Wrong   **C**   Doesn't say

24   David practised for more than a year to swim across the Cook Strait.

A   Right   **B**   Wrong   **C**   Doesn't say

25   David was in New Zealand for a long time before he swam across the Cook Strait.

A   Right   **B**   Wrong   **C**   Doesn't say

26   David's wife was in the boat beside him when he swam the Cook Strait.

A   Right   **B**   Wrong   **C**   Doesn't say

27   David had to stop for a short time while swimming the Cook Strait.

A   Right   **B**   Wrong   **C**   Doesn't say

PART 5

QUESTIONS 28–35

Read the article about doing homework.

Choose the best word (A, B or C) for each space.

For questions 28–35, mark A, B or C on your answer sheet.

Doing homework

It is a good idea to **(0)** .... your homework early. If you can do it **(28)** .... your evening meal, you will have **(29)** .... time later to do things that you enjoy, like talking **(30)** .... the phone.

It is also better to do homework as soon as possible after the teacher has given it to you. Then, if the homework is difficult and you **(31)** .... time to think about it, you will **(32)** .... have time to do it.

Always turn off your mobile phone and the television when you **(33)** .... doing homework. You will work a lot **(34)** .... without them. Make sure you have a quiet place to work, with **(35)** .... light and a comfortable chair.

Example:

| 0 | **A** starting | **B** started | **C** start | *Answer:* | 0 | A B C ☐☐■ |

28　**A**　since　　　**B**　before　　　**C**　until

29　**A**　more　　　**B**　much　　　**C**　most

30　**A**　by　　　　**B**　at　　　　**C**　on

31　**A**　should　　**B**　need　　　**C**　must

32　**A**　still　　　**B**　yet　　　　**C**　already

33　**A**　have　　　**B**　are　　　　**C**　were

34　**A**　fastest　　**B**　fast　　　**C**　faster

35　**A**　enough　　**B**　all　　　　**C**　many

PART 6

QUESTIONS 36–40

Read the descriptions of some things you can find in a kitchen.
What is the word for each one?
The first letter is already there. There is one space for each other letter in the word.
For questions 36–40, write the words on your answer sheet.

Example:

0   Breakfast, lunch and dinner are all examples of this.   m __ __ __

	Answer:	**0**	m e a l

---

36   This keeps food and drink cold.   f __ __ __ __ __

37   You use this to cut things.   k __ __ __ __

38   You do this to water to make it hot enough for a cup of coffee.   b __ __ __

39   Some people put this in their drinks to make them sweet.   s __ __ __ __

40   You can make chips with this vegetable.   p __ __ __ __ __

PART 7

QUESTIONS 41–50

Complete the letter.
Write ONE word for each space.
For questions 41–50, write the words on your answer sheet.

Example: | 0 | *f o r* |

Dear Giulia,

Thank you **(0)** .... the lovely birthday present. I already had some CDs

by the same singer but I didn't have **(41)** .... one. I like it

(42) .... much.

I **(43)** .... a lovely time on my birthday. My parents took me

(44) .... a Japanese restaurant for lunch. The food was excellent and

(45) .... all enjoyed it. **(46)** .... were some famous actors sitting

near to **(47)** .... table. I asked **(48)** .... to write their names on my

menu. They wrote: 'To Sunniya with love on your birthday'. It was

(49) .... great day. I'll **(50)** .... forget meeting them.

Love,

Sunniya

PART 8

QUESTIONS 51–55

Read the advertisement and the email.

Fill in the information in Anna's notes.

For questions 51–55, write the information on your answer sheet.

Cinemax Cinema

Monday 8 – Sunday 14 June

BLUE JUICE

4.30 pm | 7.15 pm | 8.30 pm

Moon Race

3.45 pm | 8.45 pm

Tickets: £4.75
£5.50 for films after 6 pm

| From: | Jed |
| To: | Anna |

Can you book our tickets? I'm working Friday evening but can go on Saturday. I don't want to see Blue Juice – I think the other film is better. Shall we go at the later time? Then we can eat before it starts. I'll wait for you in the café opposite at 7.30.

Anna's notes
Cinema visit

Name of cinema:	Cinemax
Name of film:	**51**
Day:	**52**
Start time:	**53** _____ pm
Cost per person:	**54** £
Place to meet Jed:	**55**

PART 9

QUESTION 56

Your friend Sam is coming to your house tomorrow evening.
Write a note to Sam.

Tell Sam:

- **what** time to come

- **what** to bring

- **how** to get to your house.

Write 25–35 words.
Write the note on your answer sheet.

PAPER 2 LISTENING (approximately 30 minutes including 8 minutes transfer time)

PART 1

QUESTIONS 1–5

You will hear five short conversations.
You will hear each conversation twice.
There is one question for each conversation.
For questions 1–5, put a tick (✓) under the right answer.

Example:

0 How many people were at the meeting?

3	13	30
☐	☐	☑

---

1 What must the man turn off?

☐	☐	☐

2 Where's the girl's pen?

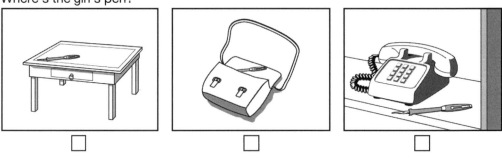

☐	☐	☐

3   What will the boy do this evening?

☐   ☐   ☐

4   What animals did they see on their holiday?

☐   ☐   ☐

5   What does the man want to buy?

  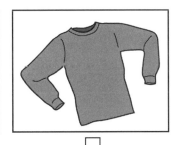

☐   ☐   ☐

PART 2

QUESTIONS 6–10

Listen to David and Eva talking about a school art lesson.
Where did they and their friends go to draw their pictures?
For questions 6–10, write a letter A–H next to each person.
You will hear the conversation twice.

Example:

0	David	E

People

6 Eva

7 Luke

8 Mary

9 Patrick

10 Cristina

Places

A bank

B café

C castle

D market

E museum

F park

G river

H swimming pool

PART 3

QUESTIONS 11–15

Listen to Dawn talking about her trip to California.
For questions 11–15, tick (✓) A, B or C.
You will hear the conversation twice.

Example:

0	Dawn went to California	**A**	last week.	☐
		B	last month.	☑
		C	last year.	☐

11	Dawn booked the concert ticket	**A**	on the internet.	☐
		B	over the phone.	☐
		C	by post.	☐

12	Dawn's plane ticket cost	**A**	£230.	☐
		B	£300.	☐
		C	£350.	☐

13	Dawn stayed in	**A**	a student hotel.	☐
		B	a family friend's home.	☐
		C	a campsite.	☐

14 Dawn thought the concert was

    A not very good. ☐

    B too short. ☐

    C too noisy. ☐

15 Most of the time, Dawn was

    A on the beach. ☐

    B on a tour bus. ☐

    C in the shops. ☐

PART 4

QUESTIONS 16–20

You will hear André telling a friend about his tennis lessons.
Listen and complete questions 16–20.
You will hear the conversation twice.

André's tennis lessons

Teacher's name:	Paul
Day:	**16**
Cost:	**17** £ .... per hour
At tennis courts in:	**18** .... Street
Starting time:	**19** .... pm
Wear:	**20** .... and T-shirt

PART 5

QUESTIONS 21–25

You will hear someone talking on the radio about a hotel in Ireland.

Listen and complete questions 21–25.

You will hear the information twice.

Hotel in Ireland

Best time to visit: June

Name: **21** The .... Hotel

Where: **22** .... Island

Hotel first built in the year: **23**

Number of bedrooms: **24**

Restaurant famous for: **25**

You now have 8 minutes to write your answers on the answer sheet.

PAPER 3   SPEAKING (8–10 minutes)

The Speaking test lasts 8 to 10 minutes. You will take the test with another candidate. There are two examiners, but only one of them will talk to you. The examiner will ask you questions and ask you to talk to the other candidate.

Part 1 (5–6 minutes)

The examiner will ask you and your partner some questions. These questions will be about your daily life, past experience and future plans. For example, you may have to speak about your school, job, hobbies or home town.

Part 2 (3–4 minutes)

You and your partner will speak to each other. You will ask and answer questions. The examiner will give you a card with some information on it. The examiner will give your partner a card with some words on it. Your partner will use the words on the card to ask you questions about the information you have. Then you will change roles.

Test 2

PAPER 1   READING AND WRITING (1 hour 10 minutes)

PART 1

QUESTIONS 1–5

Which notice (A–H) says this (1–5)?
For questions 1–5, mark the correct letter A–H on your answer sheet.

Example:

0   You must not take photographs in here.   *Answer:*

0	A	B	C	D	E	F	G	H
	□	□	□	□	□	□	□	■

---

1   Do not leave any food here.

A
> **School Trip to the Sea**
> *Don't forget your picnic!*

2   Do not leave your suitcases in front of the doors.

B
> **City Airport**
> Please keep exits free from luggage

C
> **INGHAM COUNTRY PARK**
> After eating, take your picnic things home

3   You can write to people from here.

D
> **Please write your name and address on all your suitcases**

4   Do not bring your own sandwiches here.

E
> *Internet Café*
> *Send emails, surf the net*
> *£2 per hour*

5   Be very careful to watch your bags and suitcases.

F
> **Central Station**
> Keep your luggage with you at all times

G
> **Pietro's Café**
> Please only eat food you have bought here

H
> **SOUTHPORT ART MUSEUM**
> Sorry, <u>no</u> cameras

PART 2

QUESTIONS 6–10

Read the sentences about Ingrid's home.
Choose the best word (A, B or C) for each space.
For questions 6–10, mark A, B or C on your
answer sheet.

Example:

0   Ingrid lives in a flat on the seventh .... of a large, modern building.

A   floor   **B**   line   **C**   platform   *Answer:* | 0 | A B C |

---

6   Ingrid likes living .... above the city streets.

A   tall   **B**   high   **C**   long

7   Ingrid was born in the countryside, but she .... living in the city.

A   hopes   **B**   wants   **C**   prefers

8   It only .... Ingrid ten minutes to walk from the flat to her school.

A   uses   **B**   takes   **C**   needs

9   When the lift isn't .... Ingrid has to walk up the stairs to her flat!

A   arriving   **B**   climbing   **C**   working

10   When she gets home, her mother cooks a big ....

A   meal   **B**   dish   **C**   food

PART 3

QUESTIONS 11–15

Complete the five conversations.

For questions 11–15, mark A, B or C on your answer sheet.

Example:

0

Where do you come from?

A New York.

B School.

C Home.

Answer:

0	A	B	C
	■	☐	☐

---

11 I like your new dress.

    A Do you really?

    B What's it like?

    C Do you think so?

12 How did you get to Portugal?

    A It was £50.

    B Last week.

    C By plane.

13 I'm sorry I'm late.

    A You can't go.

    B That's all right.

    C There isn't time.

14 Hello. Can I speak to Jane, please?

    A Can I leave a message?

    B I'll try again later.

    C Can I ask who's calling?

15 Remember to buy some coffee!

    A I won't forget.

    B I don't mind.

    C I'm certain, thank you.

QUESTIONS 16–20

Complete the conversation.
What does Sara say to her father?
For questions 16–20, mark the correct letter A–H on your answer sheet.

Example:

Father: Hi Sara. Did you have a good day at school?

Sara: 0 ....**G**................   *Answer:*

	A B C D E F G H
0	☐☐☐☐☐☐■☐

Father: Good, thanks. I played a game of golf.

Sara: 16 ....

Father: Oh! Why was that?

Sara: 17 ....

Father: Oh well. Did you play tennis this afternoon?

Sara: 18 ....

Father: Good for you! We must have a game at the weekend.

Sara: 19 ....

Father: Good idea. Would you like to go now?

Sara: 20 ....

Father: OK. Dinner will be ready at 7, so we can go at about 8.

A Our teacher said we needed it – but it was so boring.

B OK. But why don't we play today?

C Where did you play?

D Mm, I should do my homework first. Let's go later.

E You're lucky! We had an extra maths lesson.

F I did. It was really good. I won all my games!

G Not bad. How was your day?

H Then we can have dinner after our game.

PART 4

QUESTIONS 21–27

Read the article about two strange meetings.
Are sentences 21–27 'Right' (A) or 'Wrong' (B)?
If there is not enough information to answer 'Right' (A) or 'Wrong' (B), choose 'Doesn't say' (C).
For questions 21–27, mark A, B or C on your answer sheet.

We meet twice

My name is Anna King and I was born in a small town called Madison in Wyoming in the centre of the USA. When I was twenty, I moved to the east coast, to a town just south of New York, to start a job in a department store. One day, a young man with short brown hair who was shopping in the store looked at me and asked, 'Are you Michelle Golden?'

'No,' I said. 'But do you mean Michelle Golden from Madison?' He did. I told him that I was at school with Michelle. She wasn't much older than me and people often said that we looked just like each other. Then the young man told me that Michelle was in the same history class at university as he was.

Six months later, I got a better job with another department store and moved to the west coast to work at their San Francisco store. One day on my way home from work, a young man with short brown hair passed me in the street and asked, 'Are you Michelle Golden?'

'No,' I answered. 'You asked me that when we met in a shop several thousand miles away, near New York.'

Example:

0   Anna was born in a large town.

    A   Right   **B**   Wrong   **C**   Doesn't say   *Answer:*

	A	B	C
0	☐	■	☐

---

21   Anna left home and began working in a department store.

    A   Right   **B**   Wrong   **C**   Doesn't say

22   The young man who spoke to Anna wanted to buy a new jacket.

    A   Right   **B**   Wrong   **C**   Doesn't say

23   Anna was younger than Michelle.

    A   Right   **B**   Wrong   **C**   Doesn't say

24   Michelle and the young man were students together.

    A   Right   **B**   Wrong   **C**   Doesn't say

25   Anna got a job with the same company in San Francisco.

    A   Right   **B**   Wrong   **C**   Doesn't say

26   Anna was at work when she met the young man for the second time.

    A   Right   **B**   Wrong   **C**   Doesn't say

27   Anna was angry when the young man spoke to her a second time.

    A   Right   **B**   Wrong   **C**   Doesn't say

PART 5

QUESTIONS 28–35

Read the article about tigers.

Choose the best word (**A**, **B** or **C**) for each space.

For questions **28–35**, mark **A**, **B** or **C** on your answer sheet.

Tigers

Tigers are the **(0)** .... cats of all. A hundred years ago 100,000 tigers lived across Asia, but today **(28)** .... are only about 6000, with **(29)** .... living in zoos around the world.

Tigers usually live in forests but **(30)** .... are found in wetter areas. Most of them live **(31)** .... 12 to 18 years, but in zoos they can live **(32)** .... they are 25. The coats of **(33)** .... beautiful animals are orange and black but, surprisingly, no two coats are ever the **(34)** .... They look for food at night, and will eat fish and birds as well as larger animals.

Tigers are different from most cats because they like water. They are strong swimmers, and often go into rivers when the weather gets **(35)** .... hot.

Example:

0	**A** large	**B** larger	**C** largest		*Answer:*	

---

28 **A** that **B** it **C** there

29 **A** much **B** many **C** any

30 **A** each **B** every **C** some

31 **A** from **B** in **C** through

32 **A** during **B** until **C** above

33 **A** these **B** those **C** this

34 **A** same **B** one **C** other

35 **A** such **B** too **C** enough

PART 6

QUESTIONS 36–40

Read the descriptions of some things people often carry with them in their bags or pockets.
What is the word for each one?
The first letter is already there. There is one space for each other letter in the word.
For questions 36–40, write the words on your answer sheet.

Example:

0   If you drive a car, you should carry this with you.   l _ _ _ _ _ _

Answer: | **0** | licence |

---

36   People often write their appointments in this.   d _ _ _ _

37   Some people wear these so they can see better.   g _ _ _ _ _ _

38   You will need to keep this with you when you travel by train.   t _ _ _ _ _

39   You can read about famous people in this and it also
          has lots of pictures.   m _ _ _ _ _ _ _

40   Many people keep their money inside this.   w _ _ _ _ _

PART 7

QUESTIONS 41–50

Complete the email.
Write ONE word for each space.
For questions 41–50, write the words on your answer sheet.

Example: | **0** | *f o r*

From:	Margaret
To:	Lidija

Thank you **(0)** .... letting me stay **(41)** .... you in Ljubljana last
week. Slovenia's a great country and **(42)** .... was really nice to spend
a **(43)** .... days with you and your family. I learned so **(44)** .... about
Slovenian cooking from your mother!

I really enjoyed meeting your friends **(45)** .... the university too. Please say
hello to all of **(46)** ....

I **(47)** .... like to come back to Slovenia. If I do that, I'll make sure I can
speak more **(48)** .... your language. What **(49)** .... the best Slovene
textbook?

I **(50)** .... everyone in your family is well.

PART 8

QUESTIONS 51–55

Read the advertisement and the email.

Fill in the information in Marco's notes.

For questions 51–55, write the information on your answer sheet.

CAMP BELLAMY

SPRING ACTIVITIES

Climbing	Sailing
(Ages 13–16)	(Ages 17–19)
£60	£80

Times: 8.30 am or 2.30 pm

Courses begin:
14 April and 21 April

From: Connor

To: Marco

I've booked us on the climbing course in the afternoon at Camp Bellamy because we're not old enough to go sailing.

I know you're on holiday until 15 April, so we will start on 21 April. You need to bring some food with you but we are given special shoes when we arrive.

Marco's notes
Spring activities

Name of camp: *Camp Bellamy*

Activity booked: **51**

Start date: **52**

Time: **53**

Price per person: **54** £

Take: **55**

PART 9

QUESTION 56

You have just started a new summer job.
Write an email to your English friend, Pat.

Say:

- **what** your new job is

- **which days** you work

- **why** you like it.

Write 25–35 words.
Write the email on your answer sheet.

PAPER 2 LISTENING (approximately 30 minutes including 8 minutes transfer time)

PART 1

QUESTIONS 1–5

You will hear five short conversations.
You will hear each conversation twice.
There is one question for each conversation.
For questions 1–5, put a tick (✓) under the right answer.

Example:

0   How many people were at the meeting?

3	**13**	**30**
☐	☐	✓

---

1   Which day is the man's appointment?

Thursday	Friday	Monday
☐	☐	☐

2   What is the woman going to eat?

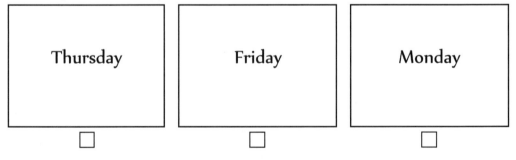

☐	☐	☐

3   Which train will the woman take?

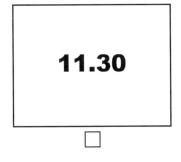

11.30

☐

12.45

☐

2.15

☐

4   How much did the man pay for the camera?

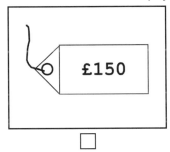

£150

☐

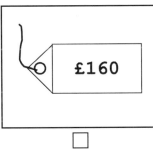

£160

☐

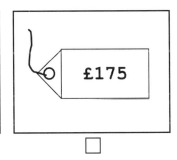

£175

☐

5   Which race did the girl win?

☐

☐

☐

PART 2

QUESTIONS 6–10

Listen to Rosie talking to a friend about places for a party.
What is the problem with each place?
For questions 6–10, write a letter A–H next to each place.
You will hear the conversation twice.

Example:

0   University Hotel   G

Places

6   Brown's Café

7   Rivers Hotel

8   Bridge Restaurant

9   Garden House

10   Opera Café

Problems

A   closed

B   cold

C   dark

D   dirty

E   expensive

F   full

G   old

H   small

PART 3

QUESTIONS 11–15

Listen to Joe asking about a French language course.
For questions 11–15, tick (✓) A, B or C.
You will hear the conversation twice.

Example:

0	Lessons for beginners are on	A	Monday.	☐
		B	Wednesday.	✓
		C	Friday.	☐

11	The best class for Joe is	A	French Conversation.	☐
		B	Business French.	☐
		C	French for Tourists.	☐

12	Joe's class begins at	A	6.30.	☐
		B	7.15.	☐
		C	8.30.	☐

13	How many other students will there be in Joe's class?	A	9	☐
		B	14	☐
		C	15	☐

14 What should Joe take to his first class?

    A a dictionary ☐

    B a coursebook ☐

    C a notebook ☐

15 Joe will pay

    A £25. ☐

    B £145. ☐

    C £170. ☐

PART 4

QUESTIONS 16–20

You will hear a girl asking for information about going to Kendal by bus.
Listen and complete questions 16–20.
You will hear the conversation twice.

Bus to Kendal

First bus leaves at: *6.45 am*

Cost of single ticket: **16**   £

Buy ticket from: **17**

Address of bus station: **18**   .... *Street*

next to: **19**

At bus station, you can buy: **20**   .... *and newspapers*

PART 5

QUESTIONS 21–25

You will hear a telephone message about a trip to the theatre.
Listen and complete questions 21–25.
You will hear the information twice.

☎ Telephone message ☎

To: Jamie

From: Michael

Name of play:	**21**	The .... Party
Date:	**22**	.... August
The theatre is opposite:	**23**	the ....
Meet Michael at:	**24**	.... pm
Mobile number:	**25**	

You now have 8 minutes to write your answers on the answer sheet.

PAPER 3   SPEAKING (8–10 minutes)

The Speaking test lasts 8 to 10 minutes. You will take the test with another candidate. There are two examiners, but only one of them will talk to you. The examiner will ask you questions and ask you to talk to the other candidate.

Part 1 (5–6 minutes)

The examiner will ask you and your partner some questions. These questions will be about your daily life, past experience and future plans. For example, you may have to speak about your school, job, hobbies or home town.

Part 2 (3–4 minutes)

You and your partner will speak to each other. You will ask and answer questions. The examiner will give you a card with some information on it. The examiner will give your partner a card with some words on it. Your partner will use the words on the card to ask you questions about the information you have. Then you will change roles.

Test 3

PAPER 1   READING AND WRITING (1 hour 10 minutes)

PART 1

QUESTIONS 1–5

Which notice (A–H) says this (1–5)?
For questions 1–5, mark the correct letter A–H on your answer sheet.

Example:

0   You can leave your luggage here.

Answer:

0	A	B	C	D	E	F	G	H
	☐	☐	☐	☐	■	☐	☐	☐

---

1   Some lorries cannot go under this.

A
> Western Railway
> Woodville Town – Drayton Park
> Monday – Friday only

2   You cannot travel by these trains at the weekend.

B
> Bus to City Centre
> Adults £1.50
> Children under 2 travel free

C
> ALL DRIVERS!
> BRIDGE ONLY 5 METRES HIGH

3   You must pay to leave your car here.

D
> Airport Bus
> 5 am – 11.30 pm daily
> £11 return

4   Use this if you have to catch a plane.

E
> City Trains
> Please put large bags
> between seats

F
> Hospital Parking
> for visitors
> £2 per hour

5   You may sit where you like.

G
> Choose any seat on the plane
> No numbers on tickets

H
> Drive Slowly
> Lorries Turning

PART 2

QUESTIONS 6–10

Read the sentences about an ice-hockey player.
Choose the best word (A, B or C) for each space.
For questions 6–10, mark A, B or C on your answer
sheet.

Example:

0   Neil .... to play ice-hockey even when he was a very small boy.

   A   enjoyed   **B**   wanted   **C**   welcomed   *Answer:*   **0**   [A ☐ B ■ C ☐]

---

6   Neil .... ice-hockey every evening with his team.

   A   made   **B**   joined   **C**   practised

7   Neil was an excellent player and his team soon began to .... competitions.

   A   earn   **B**   win   **C**   take

8   Sometimes it was .... for Neil to find enough time for both his ice-hockey and homework.

   A   difficult   **B**   terrible   **C**   worse

9   When he .... school at sixteen, Neil went to a special sports college.

   A   moved   **B**   left   **C**   passed

10   Now Neil is a famous ice-hockey player and you can often .... him on television.

   A   listen   **B**   see   **C**   look

PART 3

QUESTIONS 11–15

Complete the five conversations.
For questions 11–15, mark A, B or C on your answer sheet.

Example:

0

Where do you
come from?

A New York.

B School.

C Home.

Answer: | 0 |

---

11 Is there any sugar?

    A   Nothing.

    B   I need it.

    C   I'm afraid not.

12 Let's go to the concert tonight.

    A   Have you got tickets?

    B   Who was playing?

    C   What's it about?

13 Can you carry these bags?

    A   It doesn't matter.

    B   I'm fine, thanks.

    C   Well, I'll try.

14 Thanks for a lovely meal.

    A   I enjoyed seeing you.

    B   I'll be ready soon.

    C   I don't want to come.

15 How is your mother?

    A   She's 54.

    B   Much better, thanks.

    C   She's tall and beautiful.

QUESTIONS 16–20

Complete the conversation between two friends.
What does Anita say to Ivan?
For questions 16–20, mark the correct letter A–H on your answer sheet.

Example:

Ivan: Hi Anita. How was your weekend?

Anita: **0** ....**E**...............

Answer:

		A	B	C	D	E	F	G	H
0		☐	☐	☐	☐	■	☐	☐	☐

Ivan: OK, but I had a bit of a problem on Saturday.

Anita: **16** ....

Ivan: In a way. I couldn't find my keys.

Anita: **17**...........................

Ivan: Only to the shops. I needed a birthday present for my mum.

Anita: **18**...........................

Ivan: I bought some chocolates from the local shop. Do you think that'll be OK?

Anita: **19**...........................

Ivan: I hope so! I found my car keys this morning. They were in the bathroom.

Anita: **20**...........................

Ivan: Yes, so I can drive you home, if you like.

A   She'll love them.

B   Did you want to go anywhere special?

C   How did they get there?

D   Well, at least you've got them now.

E   Great, thanks. What about yours?

F   Did you have trouble with your car again?

G   She'll help you find them.

H   So did you get her anything in the end?

PART 4

QUESTIONS 21–27

Read the article about Ravi Patra, who works on music programmes on television, and then answer the questions.

For questions 21–27, mark A, B or C on your answer sheet.

Ravi Patra

In 2006, Ravi Patra started working for a music company and three years later, in 2009, got a job on the music television channel Rock TV.

Ravi enjoys working on television, but when he was younger he wanted to fly planes. Later, he became more interested in football. But Ravi has always loved music, so he tried to get work with Rock TV. His boss says he gave him the job because he wanted it more than anybody else!

When he started at Rock TV, Ravi arrived first at the office and was the last to leave at 10 in the evening. Now, he starts a bit later, but he is still busy until 10 pm. Before lunch, he usually writes his words for the show and in the afternoon he has meetings or makes Rock TV advertisements.

Ravi has many popular bands on his show and the stars are often interesting people. But Ravi knows that everyone watches the show to hear great music. Getting that right is more important than anything else.

Ravi knows what questions to ask the band members. He tries to make them laugh and this is easy for him. Sometimes he cannot remember their names but he always has information about the bands to help him.

Sadly, his work means that he doesn't see his friends enough, but he has great fun on skiing trips and listens to music all the time.

Example:

0	Ravi Patra started working with Rock TV in	**A**	2003.
		B	2006.
		C	2009.

Answer: 0   A B C ☐☐■

---

21 What was the first job Ravi wanted to have when he was younger?

A footballer
B pilot
C singer

22 What did Ravi's boss at Rock TV say about him?

A Ravi asked for a job at Rock TV more than once.
B There were other people better than Ravi.
C Ravi showed him how much he wanted the job.

23 How has Ravl's work changed?

A He no longer begins very early.
B He is busier than before.
C He doesn't stay late at the office.

24 In the mornings, Ravi often

A works on Rock TV advertisements.
B meets important people at his office.
C decides what to say on his programme.

25 What does Ravi think is the most important thing about the show?

A It has lots of interesting stars.
B There is great music.
C He is popular with the guests.

26 What problem does Ravi sometimes have on the Rock TV show?

A He forgets people's names.
B He cannot stop laughing.
C His questions make people angry.

27 Ravi would like to spend more time

A in the mountains.
B with his friends.
C listening to music.

PART 5

QUESTIONS 28–35

Read the article about a mountain in Japan.

Choose the best word (A, B or C) for each space.

For questions 28–35, mark A, B or C on your answer sheet.

Mount Fuji

Mount Fuji is **(0)** .... Fujisan in Japan. It is 3776 metres high and is visited **(28)** .... people from all over the world. It is a very beautiful mountain and many artists have used it in **(29)** .... work.

It is sometimes possible to see Mount Fuji from Tokyo, but often the weather is **(30)** .... cloudy to see it clearly. The **(31)** .... time to see the mountain is **(32)** .... the colder months of the year, and **(33)** .... the early morning and late evening.

A very pleasant place to enjoy Mount Fuji from is Fuji Five Lake (Fujigoko), **(34)** .... is just north of the mountain. Mount Fuji is open for climbing in July and August, but not at **(35)** .... times of the year.

Example:

0	**A** called	**B** calling	**C** calls	*Answer:*

28   **A** by   **B** for   **C** with

29   **A** his   **B** your   **C** their

30   **A** too   **B** very   **C** only

31   **A** good   **B** better   **C** best

32   **A** since   **B** during   **C** until

33   **A** on   **B** in   **C** at

34   **A** which   **B** what   **C** where

35   **A** another   **B** both   **C** other

PART 6

QUESTIONS 36–40

Read the descriptions of some things in a bathroom.
What is the word for each one?
The first letter is already there. There is one space for each other letter in the word.
For questions 36–40, write the words on your answer sheet.

Example:

0   You can use this to tidy your hair.   c __ __ __

Answer:	**0**	c	o	m	b

---

36   People stand under this to wash themselves.   s __ __ __ __ __

37   If this is large, the bathroom will have lots of light
when it is sunny.   w __ __ __ __ __

38   People wash their hair with this.   s __ __ __ __ __ __

39   You can look at yourself in this.   m __ __ __ __ __

40   If your hands are dirty, you can wash them with this.   s __ __ __

PART 7

QUESTIONS 41–50

Complete the emails.

Write ONE word for each space.

For questions 41–50, write the words on your answer sheet.

Example: | **0** | *y o u* |

| **From:** | Danny |
| **To:** | Ali |

I heard that **(0)** .... want to sell your bike.

Is it OK **(41)** .... come and see the bike after college on Thursday? I don't

know **(42)** .... you live. **(43)** .... you give me your address? I'd also like

to know why you **(44)** .... selling it.

| **From:** | Ali |
| **To:** | Danny |

I decided to sell the old bike **(45)** .... I got a motorbike for **(46)** ....

birthday. The bike is **(47)** .... few years old but I'm sure you'll like

(48) ....

I won't be at home on Thursday – I play football then and I don't get back until

late. What about coming on Friday instead? **(49)** .... that a good day for

you?

I live at 35 Portland Road, **(50)** .... to the library.

PART 8

QUESTIONS 51–55

Read the advertisement and the email.

Fill in the information on the form.

For questions 51–55, write the information on your answer sheet.

Smith's Bookshop

Book & DVD
Language Courses

Courses:	Talking Time	Speaking Plus
	Spanish	Japanese
	French	Spanish
Prices:		
Level 1:	£28.00	£30.00
Level 2:	£32.00	£35.00

From: Tom Peters

To: Jane Brown

My French course finished last week and I've just started learning Spanish. My teacher says the Speaking Plus course is the best. She can give me Level 1 so can you order Level 2 for me at the bookshop?

I'm at work until 6 pm. Ring me there (553905) or phone me this evening on 020 7865 4436.

Smith's Bookshop
Order Form

Customer's name: Tom Peters

Daytime phone number: **51**

Course name: **52**

Language: **53**

Level: **54**

Price: **55**   £

PART 9

QUESTION 56

There is going to be a concert in the town where you live.
Write an email to your English friend, Elena

- **ask** her to come to the concert.

- tell her **when** the concert is.

- say **how much** the tickets are.

Write 25–35 words.
Write the email on your answer sheet.

PAPER 2   LISTENING (approximately 30 minutes including 8 minutes transfer time)

PART 1

QUESTIONS 1–5

You will hear five short conversations.

You will hear each conversation twice.

There is one question for each conversation.

For questions 1–5, put a tick (✓) under the right answer.

Example:

0   How many people were at the meeting?

3	13	30
☐	☐	✓

---

1   Where is the photograph now?

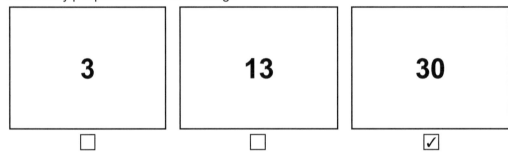

☐	☐	☐

2   When can Suzy come to dinner?

9th	**16th**	**23rd**
☐	☐	☐

3 Where did Jane go on holiday?

4 What has Maria hurt?

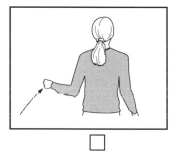      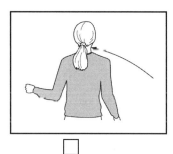

5 What time will Clare meet Jack at the station?

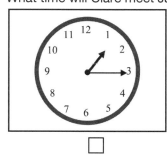   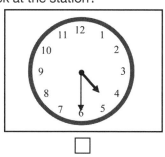   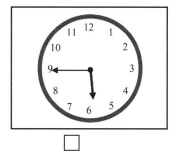

PART 2

QUESTIONS 6–10

Listen to Diana talking to a friend about the days they can do some courses.

For questions 6–10, write a letter A–H next to each day.

You will hear the conversation twice.

Example:

0   Monday

```
F
```

Days

6   Tuesday

7   Wednesday

8   Thursday

9   Friday

10   Saturday

Courses

A   Business Studies

B   Computer Studies

C   Cooking

D   Film Studies

E   Geography

F   Guitar

G   History of Art

H   The Night Sky

PART 3

QUESTIONS 11–15

Listen to a girl asking for information about a coach trip to Edinburgh.
For questions 11–15, tick (✓) A, B or C.
You will hear the conversation twice.

Example:

0	The girl wants to go to Edinburgh	**A**	this morning.	☐
		B	this afternoon.	☐
		C	tomorrow morning.	✓

11	The girl will pay	**A**	£5.	☐
		B	£7.	☐
		C	£9.	☐
12	The girl will get on the coach	**A**	outside the library.	☐
		B	in front of the Grand Hotel.	☐
		C	in Bridge Street.	☐
13	The coach will be at the girl's stop at	**A**	8.45 am.	☐
		B	8.55 am.	☐
		C	9.05 am.	☐

14 In Edinburgh, the girl will visit

    A the castle and shops. ☐

    B the cathedral and museums. ☐

    C the castle and cathedral. ☐

15 The whole trip takes

    A 2 hours. ☐

    B 2¼ hours. ☐

    C 4¼ hours. ☐

PART 4

QUESTIONS 16–20

You will hear the manager of a shop leaving a message for a customer.

Listen and complete questions 16–20.

You will hear the conversation twice.

Message for Anna

From:	*Bob Watson*
Name of shop:	**16**
Boots:	
Size:	**17**
Colour:	**18**
Sale price:	**19** £ ....
Tomorrow shop closes at:	**20**

PART 5

QUESTIONS 21–25

You will hear a man on the radio giving information about an art class.

Listen and complete questions 21–25.

You will hear the information twice.

Art class for families

Place:		Hadley College
Date:	**21**	9th ....
Start time:	**22**	.... am
Name of special guest:	**23**	J.P. ....
Price of family ticket:	**24**	£ ....
To book a place, call:	**25**	

You now have 8 minutes to write your answers on the answer sheet.

PAPER 3 SPEAKING (8–10 minutes)

The Speaking test lasts 8 to 10 minutes. You will take the test with another candidate. There are two examiners, but only one of them will talk to you. The examiner will ask you questions and ask you to talk to the other candidate.

Part 1 (5–6 minutes)

The examiner will ask you and your partner some questions. These questions will be about your daily life, past experience and future plans. For example, you may have to speak about your school, job, hobbies or home town.

Part 2 (3–4 minutes)

You and your partner will speak to each other. You will ask and answer questions. The examiner will give you a card with some information on it. The examiner will give your partner a card with some words on it. Your partner will use the words on the card to ask you questions about the information you have. Then you will change roles.

Test 4

PAPER 1   READING AND WRITING (1 hour 10 minutes)

PART 1

QUESTIONS 1–5

Which notice (A–H) says this (1–5)?

For questions 1–5, mark the correct letter A–H on your answer sheet.

Example:

0   If you need somewhere to live soon, phone
this number.

Answer:

0	A	B	C	D	E	F	G	H
	☐	☐	☐	☐	■	☐	☐	☐

---

1   If you'd like to see this place from the air,
go in the morning.

2   Use this if you are going up to one of
these apartments.

3   Phone this company if you want to go
to the airport.

4   It's possible to see this place at
different times of the day.

5   There are two ways to get tickets for this.

A
> CASTLE TOURS EVERY 2 HOURS
> TUES – SUN

B
> ***Travellers' Hotel***
> 10 km from airport
> 44 rooms

C
> Phone 552249
> to book theatre tickets
> 2pm and 8pm shows

D
> **Flight to catch?**
> Call Beach Taxis first on 242 242

E
> One-bedroom apartment
> to rent from next month
> Call 316606

F
> Park House
> This lift for apartments on floors 1–5

G
> **Helicopter flight over**
> **Dolphin Island leaves daily at 11:00**

H
> Village Concert
> pay at door or book
> tickets now on 988655

PART 2

QUESTIONS 6–10

Read the sentences about Sally's day at work.
Choose the best word (A, B or C) for each space.
For questions 6–10, mark A, B or C on your answer sheet.

Example:

0   Sally works in an office and she had a very .... day there yesterday.

    A   busy   **B**   fast   **C**   strong   *Answer:*

0	A ■	B ☐	C ☐

---

6   Sally has worked in the .... office since she left college.

    A   single   **B**   alone   **C**   same

7   Every day, Sally .... the bus to work.

    A   goes   **B**   takes   **C**   brings

8   Yesterday, Sally .... a dark blue skirt and jacket to work.

    A   had   **B**   used   **C**   wore

9   Sally .... most of her day at the office.

    A   spent   **B**   made   **C**   kept

10   Yesterday was a .... day for Sally because she had problems with her computer.

    A   difficult   **B**   tired   **C**   delayed

PART 3

QUESTIONS 11–15

Complete the five conversations.
For questions 11–15, mark A, B or C on your answer sheet.

Example:

0

Where do you come from?

A New York.

B School.

C Home.

Answer:

---

11 I'd like a cup of coffee, please.

    A Of course.

    B Yes, I do.

    C I like that.

12 Rajni's a businesswoman, isn't she?

    A Where does he work?

    B No, she can't.

    C I think so.

13 Minsk isn't in Russia.

    A Where is it then?

    B Does it have to be?

    C Isn't it somewhere?

14 Do you agree with me?

    A I haven't.

    B Certainly not.

    C No, I'm not.

15 The train has just left.

    A When did they arrive?

    B Is there another one?

    C Where are our seats?

QUESTIONS 16–20

Complete the conversation between two friends.
What does Paula say to Jenny?
For questions 16–20, mark the correct letter A–H on your answer sheet.

Example:

Jenny: It's my birthday party on Friday. Can you come?

Paula: **0** ....C.............   *Answer:* | **0** | A B C D E F G H |

Jenny: That's right – at eight o'clock. But I've got a lot to do before that.

Paula: **16** ....

Jenny: Well, you could come with me tomorrow to buy some food.

Paula: **17** ....

Jenny: That's a good idea. Shall we leave at about nine?

Paula: **18** ....

Jenny: Ten then. I'll come to your house and we'll leave when you're ready.

Paula: **19** ....

Jenny: Let's just buy pizza and cakes. Something quick and easy.

Paula: **20** ....

Jenny: See you tomorrow then.

A   I have to study first. How about a bit later?

B   Good idea! Everyone likes those

C   I'd love to. Is it in the evening?

D   If you like. Do you want to go in my car?

E   Yes, I'll be there at ten.

F   What do we need to get?

G   I'm afraid I'm at work that day.

H   Would you like me to help?

PART 4

QUESTIONS 21–27

Read the article about a basketball player called Susanna Brightman.

Are sentences 21–27 'Right' (A) or 'Wrong' (B)?

If there is not enough information to answer 'Right' (A) or 'Wrong' (B), choose 'Doesn't say' (C).

For questions 21–27, mark A, B or C on your answer sheet.

Susanna Brightman

Susanna Brightman is a young Australian basketball player. She is 195 cm tall, and very fast and strong. Some people say she may become the best player in the world one day. As well as playing for her own country, she plays for a team called *Boston Hawks* in America.

Susanna was born on 15th June 1992. Her mother and father were both basketball players and when she was just 2 weeks old she was already travelling around the country with them while they played basketball. When she was still very young, Susanna told her parents she wanted to play for Australia. At the age of 16, she played for her country for the first time.

But things have not always been easy. When Susanna was 12, she toured Australia for the first time. One day, the team she was playing for lost an important match because Susanna didn't want to play. Susanna's parents were angry with her but told her that she didn't have to play basketball if she didn't want to. She needed to think hard about her future. Luckily, Susanna decided she wanted to be a basketball player after all, and since then she has worked very hard to become an even better player.

Example:

0   Susanna Brightman comes from Australia.

    A   Right   **B**   Wrong   **C** Doesn't say   *Answer:*

0	A	B	C
	■	☐	☐

---

21   Some people think Susanna is the best basketball player in the world today.

    A   Right   **B**   Wrong   **C** Doesn't say

22   Susanna has won an important competition with *Boston Hawks.*

    A   Right   **B**   Wrong   **C** Doesn't say

23   Susanna's parents stopped playing basketball when Susanna was born.

    A   Right   **B**   Wrong   **C** Doesn't say

24   Susanna first became interested in playing basketball when she was a little child.

    A   Right   **B**   Wrong   **C** Doesn't say

25   Susanna's parents asked her to stop playing basketball when she was 12.

    A   Right   **B**   Wrong   **C** Doesn't say

26   Susanna gets angry when her team loses.

    A   Right   **B**   Wrong   **C** Doesn't say

27   Susanna knows what she wants to do with her life.

    A   Right   **B**   Wrong   **C** Doesn't say

PART 5

QUESTIONS 28–35

Read the article about kites and their history.

Choose the best word (A, B or C) for each space.

For questions 28–35, mark A, B or C on your answer sheet.

Kites

No one knows **(0)** .... made the first kite. Some people say **(28)** .... was Archytas. He was interested in mathematics and lived in Greece 2400 years ago.

But perhaps people in China flew kites long **(29)** .... then. Flying kites has always been an important part of Chinese life. The ninth day of the ninth month is a special day that is called 'The Feast of High Flight' and the sky is full **(30)** .... kites. **(31)** .... look like fish or birds and **(32)** .... the family joins in the fun.

Kites have a lot of different uses. Scientists used them in the 18th century **(33)** .... learn about storms and other kinds of weather. At the end of the 19th century, before **(34)** .... were aeroplanes, a kite that was 11 metres long **(35)** .... a man 30 metres up into the air!

Example:

0	**A**	who	**B**	why	**C**	when

Answer:

0	A ■	B ☐	C ☐

---

28 **A** they   **B** it   **C** he

29 **A** since   **B** before   **C** already

30 **A** of   **B** in   **C** from

31 **A** Both   **B** Each   **C** Some

32 **A** all   **B** other   **C** many

33 **A** for   **B** by   **C** to

34 **A** these   **B** there   **C** here

35 **A** carried   **B** carries   **C** carrying

PART 6

QUESTIONS 36–40

Read the descriptions of some words about reading and writing.

What is the word for each one?

The first letter is already there. There is one space for each other letter in the word.

For questions 36–40, write the words on your answer sheet.

Example:

0   You write this to your friends or family when you are
     on holiday.   **p** __ __ __ __ __ __ __

Answer: | **0** | *postcard* |

---

36   You choose from this list of food and drink
     in a restaurant.   **m** __ __ __

37   You look in this if you want to know what a word means.   **d** __ __ __ __ __ __ __ __ __

38   This person may write for a newspaper or a magazine.   **j** __ __ __ __ __ __ __ __ __

39   People who like reading enjoy going to this place.   **l** __ __ __ __ __ __

40   Some people put these on when they want to
     read something.   **g** __ __ __ __ __ __ __

PART 7

QUESTIONS 41–50

Complete the email.

Write ONE word for each space.

For questions 41–50, write the words on your answer sheet.

Example: | **0** | *am* |

| From: | Jan |
| To: | Monica |

Hi Monica,

I **(0)** .... writing to give you my new address – it's 24 Clifton Road. We still live in the same city but we have just moved **(41)** .... a new house. We are **(42)** .... too far from the old house so I can still see a **(43)** .... of my friends. And it's easy to go to the shops **(44)** .... bus.

The new house is bigger **(45)** .... the old one and everyone likes **(46)** .... There are three bedrooms – mine is **(47)** .... largest. From the window I can just **(48)** .... the river.

(49) .... you have time, please come and visit us. Everyone will **(50)** .... happy to see you.

PART 8

QUESTIONS 51–55

Read the notice and the email.

Fill in the information in Brian's notes.

For questions 51–55, write the information on your answer sheet.

Hexham College

Courses

French (Monday or Friday class)
First class: 6 December

Spanish (Wednesday or Friday class)
First class: 15 December

Cost

10 weeks – Beginners £85
Advanced £95
14 weeks – Beginners £105
Advanced £125

From:	Mick
To:	Brian

Can you book me onto a beginners language course at your college? I studied French last year so I want to try Spanish this time. I'd like to do the longer course and I have football practice on Friday, so I can't do a class then.

Brian's notes
Language course

Name of college: Hexham College

Which language: **51**

Day: **52**

Start date: **53**

Number of weeks: **54**

Cost: **55** £

PART 9

QUESTION 56

Read the email from your English friend, Jools.

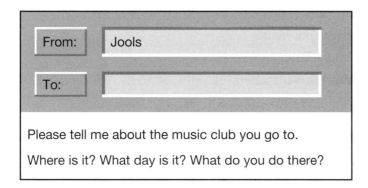

From: Jools

To:

Please tell me about the music club you go to.

Where is it? What day is it? What do you do there?

Write an email to Jools and answer the questions.

Write 25–35 words.

Write the email on your answer sheet.

PAPER 2 LISTENING (approximately 30 minutes including 8 minutes transfer time)

PART 1

QUESTIONS 1–5

You will hear five short conversations.

You will hear each conversation twice.

There is one question for each conversation.

For questions 1–5, put a tick (✓) under the right answer.

Example:

0 How many people were at the meeting?

3	**13**	**30**
☐	☐	☑

---

1 What is the man going to take to the repair shop?

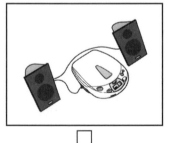 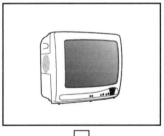 

☐ ☐ ☐

2 How will Nancy and Joe get to the sports centre?

☐ ☐ ☐

3   How much is the prize for the competition?

£100	£200	£300
☐	☐	☐

4   What will the weather be like tomorrow lunchtime?

☐   ☐   ☐

5   What time will they leave home?

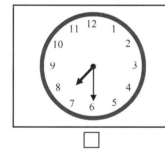  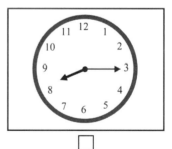

☐   ☐   ☐

PART 2

QUESTIONS 6–10

Listen to Ben talking to his wife about the clothes in his suitcase.
Which clothes will he wear each day?
For questions 6–10, write a letter A–H next to each day.
You will hear the conversation twice.

Example:

0	Sunday	D

Days

6	Monday	
7	Tuesday	
8	Wednesday	
9	Thursday	
10	Friday	

Clothes

A blue shirt

B coat

C jacket

D jeans

E light trousers

F shorts

G suit

H sweater

PART 3

QUESTIONS 11–15

Listen to Duncan talking to a friend about a tennis course.
For questions 11–15, tick (✓) A, B or C.
You will hear the conversation twice.

Example:

0	How long was the tennis course?	A	one day	☐
		B	two days	☐
		C	five days	✓

11	Duncan stayed in a hotel	A	in a town.	☐
		B	near the sea.	☐
		C	in the mountains.	☐

12	Duncan's teacher comes from	A	England.	☐
		B	France.	☐
		C	Canada.	☐

13	How much did Duncan pay for the course?	A	£185	☐
		B	£205	☐
		C	£265	☐

14 Before the course, Duncan bought himself some tennis

    A shoes. ☐

    B clothes. ☐

    C balls. ☐

15 On the last evening, there was

    A a party. ☐

    B a film show. ☐

    C a tennis match. ☐

PART 4

QUESTIONS 16–20

You will hear a woman phoning for information about a boat trip.

Listen and complete questions 16–20.

You will hear the conversation twice.

Boat trip on the River Dee

Days of boat trip:		Friday and Sunday
Get on boat at the:	**16**	
Time boat leaves:	**17**	.... pm
Boat goes to:	**18**	
On boat, you can buy:	**19**	drinks and ....
Cost of adult ticket:	**20**	£ ....

PART 5

QUESTIONS 21–25

You will hear a woman giving information on the radio about a theatre school.

Listen and complete questions 21–25.

You will hear the information twice.

Children's theatre school

Name of school:	Silver Star
Cost for children over 14:	**21** £ .... per week
Children must take their own:	**22**
There is a show every:	**23**
The first summer course starts on:	**24** 21st ....
Phone number:	**25**

You now have 8 minutes to write your answers on the answer sheet.

PAPER 3   SPEAKING (8–10 minutes)

The Speaking test lasts 8 to 10 minutes. You will take the test with another candidate. There are two examiners, but only one of them will talk to you. The examiner will ask you questions and ask you to talk to the other candidate.

Part 1 (5–6 minutes)

The examiner will ask you and your partner some questions. These questions will be about your daily life, past experience and future plans. For example, you may have to speak about your school, job, hobbies or home town.

Part 2 (3–4 minutes)

You and your partner will speak to each other. You will ask and answer questions. The examiner will give you a card with some information on it. The examiner will give your partner a card with some words on it. Your partner will use the words on the card to ask you questions about the information you have. Then you will change roles.

Visual materials for Paper 3

1A

Blue Sky International Airport
Opens next January

Cheap flights to the USA
8 miles from city centre
Car park for 2000 cars

2B

Picnic

♦ **where / picnic?**

♦ **date?**

♦ **start?** ⏲ **?**

♦ **what / take?**

♦ **music?**

3A

Fit World Sports Shop

6 Bell Street

Clothes for all sports

For adults and children

Low prices on everything

Open Monday – Saturday 9am – 5pm

4B

Job with a tour company

- ♦ **what / job?**
- ♦ **hours per day?**
- ♦ **address / company?**
- ♦ **work all year?**
- ♦ **speak other languages?**

1B

New airport

- ◆ **name / airport?**

- ◆ **where / airport?**

- ◆ **when / open?**

- ◆ **expensive flights?**

- ◆ **car park?**

2A

International College
Come to our summer picnic
in Victoria Park

Saturday 29th June

Dance to the music of
The Starmen

Starts 4pm
Please bring food

3B

Sports shop

♦ **open every day?**

♦ **address?**

♦ **sell tennis shoes?**

♦ **expensive?**

♦ **clothes / children?**

4A

Adventure Tours
4 Silver Street

We need a tour guide to work in
South America
September – March

*You must speak English and Spanish
Minimum 8 hours each day*

1C

CHEAP FLIGHTS
Internet bookings only: www.cheaptravel.com

London to Hong Kong
From £400 return
Every Monday
New planes with televisions and
computer games

2D

Restaurant

♦   **name / restaurant?**

♦   **what kind / food?**

♦   **eat outside?**

♦   **good for families?**

♦   **telephone number?**

3C

TOWN RUNNING RACE

Saturday 14th June

from Clifton Bridge
to Market Square

for adults and children over 12 years old
Great prizes –
new sports clothes and trainers

Call 848244

4D

<u>Walk for tourists</u>

♦ **where / start?**

♦ **what / visit?**

♦ **every day?**

♦ **expensive?**

♦ **lunch?**

1D

Cheap flights

♦ **where / fly to?**

♦ **cost?**

♦ **fly / weekends?**

♦ **TV / plane?**

♦ **internet address?**

2C

SUMMER PALACE RESTAURANT

The best Chinese
food in town!

*** Special meals for children ***

Also 10 tables in our pretty garden

To book a table – call 813729

3D

<u>Running race</u>

♦ **when / race?**

♦ **for everyone?**

♦ **what / win?**

♦ **where / start?**

♦ **more information? ☎ ?**

4C

City walk

Friendly guides
See the old market and castle

Starts: train station at 11am
Finishes with lunch at Park Café

On Saturdays

All for only £15

Paper 3 frames

Test 1

Note: The visual materials for Paper 3 appear on pages 96–103.

Part 1 (5–6 minutes)

Greetings and introductions

At the beginning of Part 1, the interlocutor greets the candidates, asks for their names and asks them to spell something.

Giving information about place of origin, occupation, studies

The interlocutor asks the candidates about where they come from / live, and for information about their school/studies/work.

Giving general information about self

The interlocutor asks the candidates questions about their daily life, past experience or future plans. They may be asked, for example, about their likes and dislikes or about recent past experiences, or to describe and compare places.

Extended response

In the final section of Part 1, candidates are expected to give an extended response to a 'Tell me something about . . .' prompt. The topics are still of a personal and concrete nature. Candidates should produce at least three utterances in their extended response.

Part 2 (3–4 minutes)

The interlocutor introduces the activity as follows:

Interlocutor: (*Pablo*), here is some information about a new airport.

(*Interlocutor shows answer card 1A on page 96 to Pablo.*)

(*Laura*), you don't know anything about the airport, so ask (*Pablo*) some questions about it.

(*Interlocutor shows question card 1B on page 98 to Laura.*)

Use these words to help you. (*Interlocutor indicates prompt words.*)

Do you understand?

Now, (*Laura*), ask (*Pablo*) your questions about the airport, and (*Pablo*), you answer them.

1A

1B
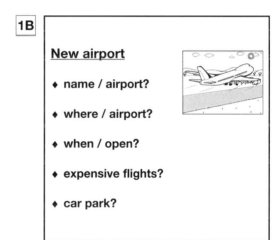

When the candidates have asked and answered questions about the airport, they exchange roles and talk about a different topic.

The interlocutor introduces the activity as follows:

Interlocutor: (*Laura*), here is some information about cheap flights.

(*Interlocutor shows answer card 1C on page 100 to Laura.*)

(*Pablo*), you don't know anything about the cheap flights, so ask (*Laura*) some questions about them.

(*Interlocutor shows question card 1D on page 102 to Pablo.*)

Use these words to help you. (*Interlocutor indicates prompt words.*)

Do you understand?

Now, (*Pablo*), ask (*Laura*) your questions about the cheap flights, and (*Laura*), you answer them.

1C

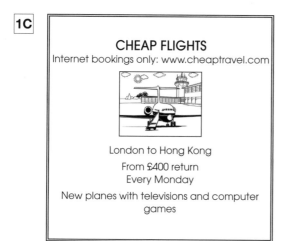

CHEAP FLIGHTS

Internet bookings only: www.cheaptravel.com

London to Hong Kong

From £400 return
Every Monday

New planes with televisions and computer games

1D

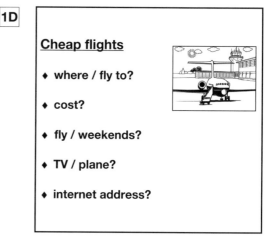

Cheap flights

♦ **where / fly to?**

♦ **cost?**

♦ **fly / weekends?**

♦ **TV / plane?**

♦ **internet address?**

Note: Candidates are assessed on both their questions and answers in Part 2 of the test.

Test 2

Note: The visual materials for Paper 3 appear on pages 96–103.

Part 1 (5–6 minutes)

Greetings and introductions

At the beginning of Part 1, the interlocutor greets the candidates, asks for their names and asks them to spell something.

Giving information about place of origin, occupation, studies

The interlocutor asks the candidates about where they come from / live, and for information about their school/studies/work.

Giving general information about self

The interlocutor asks the candidates questions about their daily life, past experience or future plans. They may be asked, for example, about their likes and dislikes or about recent past experiences, or to describe and compare places.

Extended response

In the final section of Part 1, candidates are expected to give an extended response to a 'Tell me something about . . .' prompt. The topics are still of a personal and concrete nature. Candidates should produce at least three utterances in their extended response.

Part 2 (3–4 minutes)

The interlocutor introduces the activity as follows:

Interlocutor: (*Pablo*), here is some information about a picnic.

(*Interlocutor shows answer card 2A on page 98 to Pablo.*)

(*Laura*), you don't know anything about the picnic, so ask (*Pablo*) some questions about it.

(*Interlocutor shows question card 2B on page 96 to Laura.*)

Use these words to help you. (*Interlocutor indicates prompt words.*)

Do you understand?

Now, (*Laura*), ask (*Pablo*) your questions about the picnic, and (*Pablo*), you answer them.

When the candidates have asked and answered questions about the picnic, they exchange roles and talk about a different topic.

The interlocutor introduces the activity as follows:

Interlocutor: (*Laura*), here is some information about a restaurant.

(*Interlocutor shows answer card 2C on page 102 to Laura.*)

(*Pablo*), you don't know anything about the restaurant, so ask (*Laura*) some questions about it.

(*Interlocutor shows question card 2D on page 100 to Pablo.*)

Use these words to help you. (*Interlocutor indicates prompt words.*)

Do you understand?

Now, (*Pablo*), ask (*Laura*) your questions about the restaurant, and (*Laura*), you answer them.

2C

SUMMER PALACE RESTAURANT

The best Chinese food in town!

** *Special meals for children* **

Also 10 tables in our pretty garden

To book a table – call 813729

2D

Restaurant

- ♦ **name / restaurant?**
- ♦ **what kind / food?**
- ♦ **eat outside?**
- ♦ **good for families?**
- ♦ **telephone number?**

Note: Candidates are assessed on both their questions and answers in Part 2 of the test.

Test 3

Note: The visual materials for Paper 3 appear on pages 96–103.

Part 1 (5–6 minutes)

Greetings and introductions

At the beginning of Part 1, the interlocutor greets the candidates, asks for their names and asks them to spell something.

Giving information about place of origin, occupation, studies

The interlocutor asks the candidates about where they come from / live, and for information about their school/studies/work.

Giving general information about self

The interlocutor asks the candidates questions about their daily life, past experience or future plans. They may be asked, for example, about their likes and dislikes or about recent past experiences, or to describe and compare places.

Extended response

In the final section of Part 1, candidates are expected to give an extended response to a 'Tell me something about . . .' prompt. The topics are still of a personal and concrete nature. Candidates should produce at least three utterances in their extended response.

Part 2 (3–4 minutes)

The interlocutor introduces the activity as follows:

Interlocutor: (*Pablo*), here is some information about a sports shop.

                  (*Interlocutor shows answer card 3A on page 97 to Pablo.*)

                  (*Laura*), you don't know anything about the sports shop, so ask (*Pablo*) some questions about it.

                  (*Interlocutor shows question card 3B on page 99 to Laura.*)

                  Use these words to help you. (*Interlocutor indicates prompt words*.)

                  Do you understand?

                  Now, (*Laura*), ask (*Pablo*) your questions about the sports shop, and (*Pablo*), you answer them.

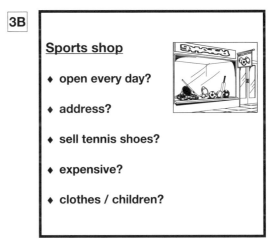

When the candidates have asked and answered questions about the sports shop, they exchange roles and talk about a different topic.

The interlocutor introduces the activity as follows:

Interlocutor: (*Laura*), here is some information about a running race.

(*Interlocutor shows answer card 3C on page 101 to Laura.*)

(*Pablo*), you don't know anything about the running race, so ask (*Laura*) some questions about it.

(*Interlocutor shows question card 3D on page 103 to Pablo.*)

Use these words to help you. (*Interlocutor indicates prompt words.*)

Do you understand?

Now, (*Pablo*), ask (*Laura*) your questions about the running race, and (*Laura*), you answer them.

3C

TOWN RUNNING RACE

Saturday 14th June

from Clifton Bridge
to Market Square

for adults and children over 12 years old
Great prizes –
new sports clothes and trainers

Call 848244

3D

Running race

♦ **when / race?**

♦ **for everyone?**

♦ **what / win?**

♦ **where / start?**

♦ **more information? ☎ ?**

Note: Candidates are assessed on both their questions and answers in Part 2 of the test.

Test 4

Note: The visual materials for Paper 3 appear on pages 96–103.

Part 1 (5–6 minutes)

Greetings and introductions

At the beginning of Part 1, the interlocutor greets the candidates, asks for their names and asks them to spell something.

Giving information about place of origin, occupation, studies

The interlocutor asks the candidates about where they come from / live, and for information about their school/studies/work.

Giving general information about self

The interlocutor asks the candidates questions about their daily life, past experience or future plans. They may be asked, for example, about their likes and dislikes or about recent past experiences, or to describe and compare places.

Extended response

In the final section of Part 1, candidates are expected to give an extended response to a 'Tell me something about . . .' prompt. The topics are still of a personal and concrete nature. Candidates should produce at least three utterances in their extended response.

Part 2 (3–4 minutes)

The interlocutor introduces the activity as follows:

Interlocutor: (*Pablo*), here is some information about a job with a tour company.

                  (*Interlocutor shows answer card 4A on page 99 to Pablo.*)

                  (*Laura*), you don't know anything about the job with the tour company, so ask (*Pablo*) some questions about it.

                  (*Interlocutor shows question card 4B on page 97 to Laura.*)

                  Use these words to help you. (*Interlocutor indicates prompt words.*)

                  Do you understand?

                  Now, (*Laura*), ask (*Pablo*) your questions about the job, and (*Pablo*), you answer them.

4A

Adventure Tours
4 Silver Street

We need a tour guide to work in
South America
September – March

*You must speak English and Spanish
Minimum 8 hours each day*

4B

Job with a tour company

♦ **what / job?**

♦ **hours per day?**

♦ **address / company?**

♦ **work all year?**

♦ **speak other languages?**

When the candidates have asked and answered questions about the job with the tour company, they exchange roles and talk about a different topic.

The interlocutor introduces the activity as follows:

Interlocutor: (*Laura*), here is some information about a walk for tourists.

(*Interlocutor shows answer card 4C on page 103 to Laura.*)

(*Pablo*), you don't know anything about the walk for tourists, so ask (*Laura*) some questions about it.

(*Interlocutor shows question card 4D on page 101 to Pablo.*)

Use these words to help you. (*Interlocutor indicates prompt words.*)

Do you understand?

Now, (*Pablo*), ask (*Laura*) your questions about the walk for tourists, and (*Laura*), you answer them.

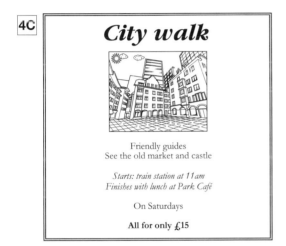

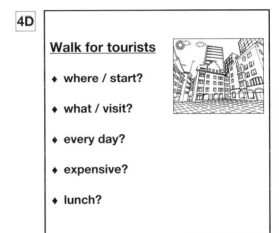

Note: Candidates are assessed on both their questions and answers in Part 2 of the test.

Test 1 Answer key

Paper 1 Reading and Writing

Part 1
1 B   **2** F   **3** D   **4** A   **5** G

Part 2
6 A   **7** C   **8** B   **9** A   **10** C

Part 3
11 B   **12** A   **13** C   **14** A   **15** C   **16** E   **17** G   **18** C   **19** H   **20** D

Part 4
21 A   **22** C   **23** A   **24** A   **25** B   **26** C   **27** B

Part 5
28 B   **29** A   **30** C   **31** B   **32** A   **33** B   **34** C   **35** A

Part 6
For questions 36–40, spelling must be correct.
36 fridge   **37** knife   **38** boil   **39** sugar/syrup   **40** potato

Part 7
For questions 41–50, ignore capitals / absence of capitals. Spelling must be correct.
41 this/that/every   **42** very/so   **43** had   **44** to   **45** we   **46** There   **47** our/my/the   **48** them   **49** a   **50** never/not

Part 8
For questions 51–55, spelling must be correct.
51 Moon Race   **52** Sat(urday)   **53** 8.45(pm)   **54** (£)5.50   **55** café (opposite)

Part 9

Question 56

The three parts of the message that must be communicated are:

i   the time Sam should come to your house
ii what Sam should bring with him/her
iii details of how to get to your house.

Sample answer A

Mark: 5

> DEAR SAM,
>
> TOMORROW YOU SHOULD ARRIVE AT 6.00p.m.
> YOU SHOULD BRING SOME MONEY FOR THE TICKET OF THE CINEMA.
> WHEN YOU ARRIVE AT THE STATION PHONE ME AND I'LL COME TO PICK
> YOU UP!
> LOVE FROM LUCA

All three parts of the message are clearly communicated.

Sample answer B

Mark: 3

> My friend Sam came to my house at 7.00 evening yesterday he bought
> his child and pasta of cake, he got my house after he asked my anther
> friend live in my street.

All three parts of the message are included but the context is incorrect (wrong time/
tense).

Sample answer C

Mark: 0

> Hi Sam!!
> I listen, you come to my house tomorrow. We playing many games. Do you
> like golf? We go to play with Tiger Wood!! Was it verry funny.
> I am wait you.

The question has not been attempted (the response does not relate to the prompts).

Sample answer D

Mark: 1

> Hi Sam!
> It is Ivan, I want ask you some questions. What time do you come to my
> house? Do you will bring any friends? How are you will be get to my house?
> I know one bus, It going from station to my house, number of this bus is a
> twnty five (25)
> Se you tomorrow.
> Bye! Ivan.

Only one part (iii) of the message is communicated.

Sample answer E

Mark: 3

> Hello Sam, you can came here at 7.00 pm You will bring some CDs and
> the book of history for study. I have bought a new stereo and I have
> tidyed my bedroom
> Aline

Two parts of the message are clearly communicated but one part (iii) is unattempted.

Paper 2   Listening

Part 1

1 A   **2** C   **3** B   **4** C   **5** C

Part 2

6 D   **7** F   **8** H   **9** A   **10** B

Part 3

11 B   **12** A   **13** B   **14** B   **15** C

Part 4

16 Wed(nesday)(s)   **17** (£)12/twelve (pounds) (a/an/per hour)
18 GERALD (Street)   **19** 6.15 / 18.15 / quarter past six (pm) / six fifteen   **20** short(s)

Part 5

21 (The) White (Hotel)   **22** ACHILL (Island)   **23** 1859 / eighteen fifty(-)nine
24 36 / thirty(-)six (bedrooms)   **25** fish/seafood

Transcript

This is the Cambridge Key English Test. Paper 2: Listening. Test number one.
There are five parts to the test: Parts One, Two, Three, Four and Five.
We will now stop for a moment before we start the test. Please ask any
questions now because you must not speak during the test.

[pause]

PART 1   *Now look at the instructions for Part One.*

[pause]

You will hear five short conversations. You will hear each conversation twice.
There is one question for each conversation. For questions 1–5, put a tick under
the right answer.
Here is an example:
How many people were at the meeting?

Woman:	Were there many people at the meeting?
Man:	About thirty.
Woman:	That's not many.
Man:	No, but more than last time.

[pause]

The answer is thirty, so there is a tick in box C.
Now we are ready to start. Look at question one.

[pause]

Question 1   *One. What must the man turn off?*

Woman:	Let's go or we'll be late. Did you turn off the lights upstairs?
Man:	Yes, but wait a minute – I can hear the radio in the kitchen.
Woman:	Oh dear. That's the television. I was watching the news. Can you go and turn it off and I'll start the car?
Man:	OK.

[pause]

Now listen again.

[repeat]

[pause]

Question 2   *Two. Where's the girl's pen?*

Girl:	Where's my blue pen? I'm sure I put it in my bag.
Boy:	Oh, sorry. I used it to do my homework and I left it on the table in the kitchen.
Girl:	I can't see it.
Boy:	Oh, I know, it's by the phone – I used it again to take a message and forgot to put it back in your bag. I'll get it for you.

[pause]

Now listen again.

[repeat]

[pause]

Question 3   *Three. What will the boy do this evening?*

Woman: Are you going to practise your guitar with your friends here this evening?

Boy: Matthew's playing in a football match tonight so we're going to do it tomorrow.

Woman: Will you wash the car for me then? It's very dirty.

Boy: Sorry, Mum, I'm going to go and watch Matthew play. I'll do the car for you at the weekend.

[pause]

Now listen again.

[repeat]

[pause]

Question 4   *Four. What animals did they see on their holiday?*

Man: Did you see any monkeys when you were on holiday in Kenya?

Woman: Lots of them! But we weren't so lucky with the lions.

Man: Oh, that's a pity! What about elephants?

Woman: Not this time, but we're going back next year so maybe we'll see some elephants then.

[pause]

Now listen again.

[repeat]

[pause]

Question 5   *Five. What does the man want to buy?*

Man: Do you think this sweater will look nice with my jacket?

Woman: The colour isn't quite right. What about that lovely blue shirt over there?

Man: It is nice, but I've got lots of shirts already. I need something warm to wear under my jacket.

Woman: Well, let's look in another shop then.

[pause]

Now listen again.

[repeat]

[pause]

This is the end of Part One.

[pause]

PART 2   *Now look at Part Two.*

[pause]

Listen to David and Eva talking about a school art lesson. Where did they and their friends go to draw their pictures? For questions 6–10, write a letter, A–H, next to each person. You will hear the conversation twice.

[pause]

David:	I really enjoyed the art lesson yesterday, Eva.
Eva:	Me too, David. I liked going into the city to draw different places. Is this your picture of the museum?
David:	Yes. What did you draw?
Eva:	I couldn't decide between the castle and the market. In the end, I did a drawing of people buying vegetables. Do you know what Luke drew?
David:	Yes, I met him in a café after the lesson. His picture was of some people in the park having a picnic.
Eva:	I know Mary loves drawing water. Did she go to the river?
David:	She went to the sports centre and drew some children having a swimming lesson. What about Patrick?
Eva:	We were walking to the market together but then he saw someone cleaning windows in the bank and he stopped to draw that.
David:	Cristina is the best artist. I saw her in Bridge Street sitting at a table having a drink. She was drawing a waiter talking to a customer. The picture looked really good.
Eva:	What a great art lesson!

[pause]

Now listen again.

[repeat]

[pause]

This is the end of Part Two.

[pause]

PART 3 *Now look at Part Three.*

[pause]

Listen to Dawn talking about her trip to California. For questions 11–15, tick A, B or C. You will hear the conversation twice. Look at questions 11–15 now. You have 20 seconds.

[pause]

Now listen to the conversation.

Man:	Hello, Dawn, I haven't seen you for weeks.
Dawn:	Well, last month I went to California for a concert.
Man:	How did you get the concert ticket?
Dawn:	My computer wasn't working, so I couldn't use the internet, and the post takes too long, so I called the ticket office and booked one that way.
Man:	Really? Was your plane ticket expensive?
Dawn:	Well, most people pay three hundred and fifty pounds, but my student ticket was only two hundred and thirty pounds. Even flights booked on the internet cost three hundred pounds.
Man:	Great! Did you stay in a student hotel?
Dawn:	I was so lucky! My mother's old schoolfriend let me use her apartment. That was nicer than going to a student place or a campsite.
Man:	Tell me about the concert.

Dawn:	Well, one group didn't come so it finished an hour early. That made me angry! But the music was great and very loud – I loved it!
Man:	Did you go to the beach?
Dawn:	Well, it was a long bus trip to get there so I only went once. Anyway, I spent most days buying clothes.
Man:	It all sounds great!

[pause]

Now listen again.

[repeat]

[pause]

This is the end of Part Three.

[pause]

PART 4   *Now look at Part Four.*

[pause]

You will hear André telling a friend about his tennis lessons. Listen and complete questions 16–20. You will hear the conversation twice.

[pause]

Girl:	Did you win your match last night, André?
André:	Yes. I'm much better since I started having tennis lessons with my new teacher, Paul.
Girl:	How often do you have lessons?
André:	Every Wednesday because the only other day he teaches is Friday and I can't go then. You like tennis. Why don't you come too?
Girl:	Hmm. How much are the lessons? That's the first question my parents will ask!
André:	I give Paul twelve pounds and he teaches me for an hour. It's not expensive.
Girl:	No. Maria pays eighteen pounds an hour.
André:	But she goes to the tennis club. Paul works at the tennis courts in Gerald Street.
Girl:	How do you spell that?
André:	G E R A L D.
Girl:	OK. And what time's your lesson? Can I come and meet Paul next time?
André:	Yes. I start at six fifteen and play until quarter past seven. You can come at the same time.
Girl:	OK. What should I wear?
André:	You don't need to wear a tennis dress. Shorts and a T-shirt will be fine.
Girl:	All right. See you then.

[pause]

Now listen again.

[repeat]

[pause]

This is the end of Part Four.

[pause]

PART 5   *Now look at Part Five.*

[pause]

You will hear someone talking on the radio about a hotel in Ireland. Listen and complete questions 21–25. You will hear the information twice.

[pause]

This week I'm going to tell you about my favourite hotel. It's in the west of Ireland and the best time to go there is June. I've loved this hotel since I was a child. It's called The White Hotel because it's always painted that colour. It's built on one of the most beautiful islands I have ever visited – Achill Island. You say 'Akil', but it's spelt A C H I double L.

It's one of the oldest hotels in this part of the country. It was built in eighteen fifty-nine and the rich and famous have enjoyed going there ever since. You can see the sea or mountains from every room. But it's difficult to book a bedroom there because there are only thirty-six of them and the hotel can't take more than fifty guests at one time.

Visitors also enjoy the hotel restaurant. People go there from all over the world to eat its fish. It's caught that day in the sea round the island. Try it cooked with tomatoes.

So, if you want . . .

[pause]

Now listen again.

[repeat]

[pause]

This is the end of Part Five.

You now have eight minutes to write your answers on the answer sheet.

Note: Teacher, stop the recording here and time eight minutes. Remind the students when there is **one** minute remaining.

[pause]

That is the end of the test.

Test 2 Answer key

Paper 1   Reading and Writing

Part 1

1 C   **2** B   **3** E   **4** G   **5** F

Part 2

6 B   **7** C   **8** B   **9** C   **10** A

Part 3

11 A   **12** C   **13** B   **14** C   **15** A   **16** E   **17** A   **18** F   **19** B   **20** D

Part 4

21 A   **22** C   **23** A   **24** A   **25** B   **26** B   **27** C

Part 5

28 C   **29** B   **30** C   **31** A   **32** B   **33** A   **34** A   **35** B

Part 6

For questions 36–40, spelling must be correct.

36 diary   **37** glasses   **38** ticket   **39** magazine   **40** wallet

Part 7

For questions 41–50, ignore capitals / absence of capitals. Spelling must be correct.

41 with   **42** it   **43** few   **44** much   **45** in/from/at   **46** them
47 would/should/'d   **48** of   **49** is/'s   **50** hope/trust

Part 8

For questions 51–55, spelling must be correct.

51 C/climbing   **52** 21(st) April   **53** 2.30 (pm) / 14.30   **54** (£)60(.00)   **55** (some) food

Part 9

Question 56

The three parts of the message that must be communicated are:

i   what your new summer job is
ii the day(s) you work
iii the reason(s) you like your job

Sample answer A

Mark: 5

> Hi Pat,
> How are you? I'm good. I've got a new job. It's teaching Japanese.
> I teach every Thursday. I like my new job because the teaching is very
> interesting for me.
> See you.
> Keiko

All three parts of the message are clearly communicated.

Sample answer B

Mark: 3

> Hello Pat,
> This summer I worked as tennis teacher in my town.
> I worked only on Monday and Saturday. I meet a lot people. I liked to do
> that because I had a lot of free time to practice all my sports.
> Cheers,
> Antonio

All three parts of the message are included but the context is incorrect (wrong time/
tense).

Sample answer C

Mark: 4

> Hello. How are you?
> I got a new job! My new job is book shop. I work the book shop on Monday,
> Tuesday, Wednesday and Sunday! I love my job! because I love books.
> I'm so happy!!

All three parts of the message are communicated but with some awkwardness of
expression.

Sample answer D

Mark: 1

> Hello! Pat. How are you. I have been listened that you have been joined a
> job is libary . It good you may have been get bored siting it the home all
> the time in summers. OK so do this work hardly and cleverly
> Your friend
> Prasad

Some attempt has been made to address the task but the response is very unclear.

Sample answer E

Mark: 2

> Dear friend
> I have a new summer job that is send the postcard
> They told me I can start work tomorrow
> I'm really like it because I can travil to many place
> What about you?
> Jia Hua

There is some relevant content to two points but the response is unclear.

Paper 2 Listening

Part 1

1 C   **2** B   **3** B   **4** B   **5** A

Part 2

6 A   **7** D   **8** F   **9** E   **10** H

Part 3

11 C   **12** A   **13** B   **14** A   **15** B

Part 4

16 (£) 18.25 / eighteen (pounds) twenty-five   **17** (the) (bus) driver
18 GATELY (Street)   **19** (the) museum   **20** (a/some) drink(s)

Part 5

21 (The) Dinner (Party)   **22** 29(th) / twenty(-)ninth   **23** (the) library
24 6.45 / 18.45 / six forty(-)five / quarter to seven (pm)   **25** 0774 32316

Transcript

This is the Cambridge Key English Test. Paper 2: Listening. Test number two.
There are five parts to the test: Parts One, Two, Three, Four and Five.
We will now stop for a moment before we start the test. Please ask any
questions now because you must not speak during the test.

[pause]

PART 1   *Now look at the instructions for Part One.*

[pause]

You will hear five short conversations. You will hear each conversation twice.
There is one question for each conversation. For questions 1–5, put a tick under
the right answer.
Here is an example:
How many people were at the meeting?

Woman:	Were there many people at the meeting?
Man:	About thirty.
Woman:	That's not many.
Man:	No, but more than last time.

[pause]

The answer is thirty, so there is a tick in box C.
Now we are ready to start. Look at question one.

[pause]

Question 1   *One. Which day is the man's appointment?*

Man:	I'd like to make an appointment to see Dr Owen tomorrow morning, please.
Woman:	That's Thursday. He's not free at all tomorrow. What about Friday afternoon? If not, it will have to be Monday morning.
Man:	I can't come any afternoon. I suppose I'll have to have the morning appointment then.
Woman:	OK, we'll see you at nine. What's your . . .

[pause]

Now listen again.

[repeat]

[pause]

Question 2   *Two. What is the woman going to eat?*

Man:	I'm going to have chicken and salad. What would you like?
Woman:	Um, the soup looks good, but the weather's a bit too warm for anything hot.
Man:	Why don't you have sandwiches?
Woman:	They don't look very nice. I think I'll have the same as you.

[pause]

Now listen again.

[repeat]

[pause]

Question 3   *Three. Which train will the woman take?*

Woman: When is the next train to Ashford?
Man: I'm afraid you're just too late for the eleven thirty. The next one is
         twelve forty-five, but you'll have to change trains. The two fifteen is
         quicker because it goes straight to Ashford.
Woman: I don't mind changing trains – I'll have a return ticket, please.
Man: There you are.

[pause]

Now listen again.

[repeat]

[pause]

Question 4   *Four. How much did the man pay for the camera?*

Man: I've bought a new camera.
Woman: It looks expensive. Cameras like that cost about a hundred and fifty
         pounds, don't they?
Man: This was a hundred and seventy-five pounds but the man in the
         shop took fifteen pounds off the price because it was in the shop
         window and there was no box for it.
Woman: A hundred and sixty pounds is still a lot of money. I hope it takes
         good pictures!

[pause]

Now listen again.

[repeat]

[pause]

Question 5   *Five. Which race did the girl win?*

Girl: Were you at the sports competition on Saturday?
Boy: Yes. I saw you come first in your bicycle race. But your best sport is
         swimming, isn't it?
Girl: Yes – but I was second in that. Next year I'm going to try running in
         the eight hundred metres too.
Boy: Wow! You *are* good at sports!

[pause]

Now listen again.

[repeat]

[pause]

This is the end of Part One.

[pause]

PART 2   *Now look at Part Two.*

[pause]

Listen to Rosie talking to a friend about places for a party. What is the problem with each place? For questions 6–10, write a letter, A–H, next to each place. You will hear the conversation twice.

[pause]

Man:	Have you found a room for your birthday party yet, Rosie?
Rosie:	Yes, at the University Hotel. It's old but the room's nice and big.
Man:	Did you look at any other places?
Rosie:	Yes, five! And there was something wrong with all of them!
Man:	Why didn't you like Brown's Café?
Rosie:	I loved it but they're putting in a new kitchen so they won't be open for two months.
Man:	Oh. And the Rivers Hotel? It was very cold when I went there last year.
Rosie:	It's quite warm now but it's not very clean!
Man:	Pity! What about the Bridge Restaurant? Or is it too dark there?
Rosie:	No, but the problem is none of their rooms is free on my birthday.
Man:	And it's expensive.
Rosie:	Not really, but the Garden House is.
Man:	Oh yes, I know! I had a great dinner party at the Opera Café last week.
Rosie:	It's fine for a dinner but it's not big enough for a party.
Man:	So, the University Hotel it is then?
Rosie:	Yes.

[pause]

Now listen again.

[repeat]

[pause]

This is the end of Part Two.

[pause]

PART 3   *Now look at Part Three.*

[pause]

Listen to Joe asking about a French language course. For questions 11–15, tick A, B or C. You will hear the conversation twice. Look at questions 11–15 now. You have 20 seconds.

[pause]

Now listen to the conversation.

Joe:	Hello. I'd like some information about French courses, please.
Woman:	Certainly. Beginners classes are on Wednesdays, other classes are on Mondays or Fridays.
Joe:	I'm a beginner and I'm going to France on holiday. I want to speak to people in shops and read information in museums and other places.
Woman:	Do 'French for Tourists' then. It'll be better than our Business class and you want more than French Conversation.

Joe:	Great. I can only come in the evening.
Woman:	Fine, it starts at half past six, there's a break at quarter past seven and you go on until half past eight.
Joe:	Is it a big class?
Woman:	We never have fewer than nine students or more than fifteen and . . . let me see, there are fourteen at the moment, so with you, the class will be full.
Joe:	OK. What about the coursebook?
Woman:	You'll get that in the first class and a special notebook. Bring a dictionary – that's always useful.
Joe:	Fine. Oh, how much is the course?
Woman:	It's a hundred and seventy pounds for people from outside the city, but it's twenty-five pounds less, or a hundred and forty-five pounds, if you live here.
Joe:	Oh, I do.
Woman:	Good. So let me just take your name . . .

[pause]

Now listen again.

[repeat]

[pause]

This is the end of Part Three.

[pause]

PART 4 *Now look at Part Four.*

[pause]

You will hear a girl asking for information about going to Kendal by bus. Listen and complete questions 16–20. You will hear the conversation twice.

[pause]

Man:	Good morning. Bus Travel Centre.
Girl:	Hello. I'm phoning about buses to Kendal. I'd like to travel there early. What time does the first bus leave?
Man:	The first Kendal bus, that's six forty-five a.m.
Girl:	And how much is a ticket?
Man:	It's eighteen pounds twenty-five for a single, and a return is twenty-six pounds.
Girl:	Will the ticket office be open so early in the morning?
Man:	No, but when you get on the bus the driver will sell you a ticket. Please have the right money for him.
Girl:	OK, fine. Can you tell me where the bus station is?
Man:	Yes, it's in Gately Street. That's G A T E L Y.
Girl:	I'm not sure where that is.
Man:	It's in the city centre. Do you know the museum? It's next to that.
Girl:	Oh yes, I know. And can I get something to eat at the station?
Man:	I'm afraid there isn't a café but there is a small shop. You can get newspapers and drinks there.
Girl:	Oh, I'll bring some sandwiches then. Thank you. Goodbye.

[pause]

Now listen again.

[repeat]

[pause]

This is the end of Part Four.

[pause]

PART 5   *Now look at Part Five.*

[pause]

You will hear a telephone message about a trip to the theatre. Listen and complete questions 21–25. You will hear the information twice.

[pause]

Hi Jamie, this is Michael. Sorry you're not in. Would you like to come to the theatre with me? There's a play on called *The Dinner Party*. It's about a group of friends who meet again after twenty-five years for a meal. People say it's really good.

    I know it's your birthday on August the twenty-seventh. Well, the play is on the twenty-ninth. I'll pay for your ticket as a birthday present if you like.

    It's in the New Theatre. It's that big building in Church Street just across the road from the library. It hasn't been open long and it's very nice and modern inside.

    The play starts at eight o'clock, so why don't we meet in the coffee bar first? I'll see you there at six forty-five and we can have a drink before it starts.

    If you'd like to come, call me on my mobile. The number's oh double seven four, three two three one six. Speak to you soon. Bye.

[pause]

Now listen again.

[repeat]

[pause]

This is the end of Part Five.

You now have eight minutes to write your answers on the answer sheet.

Note: Teacher, stop the recording here and time eight minutes. Remind the students when there is **one** minute remaining.

[pause]

That is the end of the test.

Test 3 Answer key

Paper 1   Reading and Writing

Part 1
1 C   **2** A   **3** F   **4** D   **5** G

Part 2
6 C   **7** B   **8** A   **9** B   **10** B

Part 3
11 C   **12** A   **13** C   **14** A   **15** B   **16** F   **17** B   **18** H   **19** A   **20** D

Part 4
21 B   **22** C   **23** A   **24** C   **25** B   **26** A   **27** B

Part 5
28 A   **29** C   **30** A   **31** C   **32** B   **33** B   **34** A   **35** C

Part 6
For questions 36–40, spelling must be correct.
36 shower   **37** window   **38** shampoo   **39** mirror   **40** soap

Part 7
For questions 41–50, ignore capitals / absence of capitals. Spelling must be correct.
41 to   **42** where   **43** Can/Could/Will/Would/Did   **44** are/'re
45 because/when/after/as/since/before   **46** my   **47** a
48 it/this/that   **49** Is   **50** next/close/near

Part 8
For questions 51–55, spelling must be correct.
51 553905   **52** Speaking Plus (course) (Spanish)   **53** Spanish
54 Level 2   **55** £35(.00)

Part 9
Question 56
The three parts of the message that must be communicated are:

i   your invitation to Elena to come to the concert in your town
ii details of when the concert is
iii the price of the tickets.

Sample answer A

Mark: 4

> Dear Elena
> I am Fareed. I have concert in this week. Colud you please come to the concert. the price of the tickets are £20 and the concert started From 8.00pm to 11.30p.m. you can coming with your Famley
> See you soon

All three parts of the message are communicated but with some awkwardness of expression.

Sample answer B

Mark: 5

> Hi Elena,
> Saturday night, there is a big concert in Nantes
> Do you want to go there with me?
> It starts at 8:00 pm and a ticket cost £8.
> I hope you'll come.
> See you later.

All three parts of the message are clearly communicated but with occasional grammatical errors.

Sample answer C

Mark: 1

> Hello ELENA are you allright? and, do you come to the concert of pop? when the concert take place? because I d'ont know when is it, so how much does the tickets cost?
> thank you see you soon.

Only one part of the message (i) is communicated.

Sample answer D

Mark: 1

> *Dear Elena,*
> *How are you? would you like to come to the concert near to the offic? How much the tickets?*
> *see you soon*
> *Jamal!*

Only one part (i) of the message is communicated.

Sample answer E

Mark: 2

> *Hi, Elena:*
> *We are going to be a concert in the town where you live, do you want go to be a concert? The concert is at 10:00 AM to 12:00 AM. We have 50 tickets, I will wait your answer*
> *Your frind, Victor*

Only two parts of the message are communicated and with errors requiring interpretation.

Paper 2   Listening

Part 1

1 C   **2** A   **3** B   **4** B   **5** C

Part 2

6 C   **7** D   **8** A   **9** H   **10** G

Part 3

11 B   **12** A   **13** B   **14** C   **15** C

Part 4

16 FORSTER(')S   **17** 38 / thirty(-)eight   **18** green
19 (£) 65(.00) / sixty(-)five (pounds)   **20** 2(.00) / 14.00 / two (o'clock) (pm)

Part 5

21 Oct(ober)   **22** 10.15 (am) / (a) quarter past ten / ten fifteen
23 (J.P.) HAYWARD   **24** (£)8.70 / eight (pounds) (and) seventy (p/pence)   **25** 4497 6390

This is the Cambridge Key English Test. Paper 2: Listening. Test number three.
There are five parts to the test: Parts One, Two, Three, Four and Five.
We will now stop for a moment before we start the test. Please ask any
questions now because you must not speak during the test.

[pause]

PART 1   *Now look at the instructions for Part One.*

[pause]

You will hear five short conversations. You will hear each conversation twice.
There is one question for each conversation. For questions 1–5, put a tick under
the right answer.
Here is an example:
How many people were at the meeting?

Woman: Were there many people at the meeting?
Man: About thirty.
Woman: That's not many.
Man: No, but more than last time.

[паузе]

The answer is thirty, so there is a tick in box C.
Now we are ready to start. Look at question one.

[pause]

Question 1   *One. Where is the photograph now?*

Man: Where's our photograph gone?
Woman: I put it on the wall next to the window. It didn't look good where you
            put it above the cupboard.
Man: But you can't see it by the window. Shall I put it next to the phone?
Woman: It'll fall off there. Let's leave it where it is.
Man: OK then.

[pause]

Now listen again.

[repeat]

[pause]

Question 2   *Two. When can Suzy come to dinner?*

Diane: Hello, Suzy. It's Diane. I'm just calling to see if you're free for dinner
            next Saturday, the ninth, or the Saturday after, the sixteenth.
Suzy: The ninth is fine. We're away from the sixteenth until the twenty-third.
Diane: So, next weekend then.
Suzy: Yes, that will be lovely. What time . . .

[pause]

Now listen again.

[repeat]

[pause]

135

Question 3   *Three. Where did Jane go on holiday?*

Boy:	Did you go camping again this year, Jane?
Jane:	Our tent is too old so we stayed with my Aunt Vera. She lives in an apartment by the beach. I don't like swimming but we went walking and horse riding a lot. It was great!
Boy:	Doesn't your aunt live in the mountains?
Jane:	She moved last year.

[pause]

Now listen again.

[repeat]

[pause]

Question 4   *Four. What has Maria hurt?*

Man:	Are you all right, Maria? What's wrong with your neck?
Maria:	Ah, I've just fallen over in the snow and I've got a terrible pain in my arm, not my neck.
Man:	Give me your hand and I'll help you up.
Maria:	OK. Thanks.

[pause]

Now listen again.

[repeat]

[pause]

Question 5   *Five. What time will Clare meet Jack at the station?*

Clare:	What time will you arrive at the station, Jack? I'll come and meet you.
Jack:	Well, Clare, the train leaves London at half past four.
Clare:	So you should be here at quarter to six.
Jack:	That's right. It takes one hour and fifteen minutes.

[pause]

Now listen again.

[repeat]

[pause]

That is the end of Part One.

[pause]

PART 2   *Now look at Part Two.*

[pause]

Listen to Diana talking to a friend about the days they can do some courses. For questions 6–10, write a letter, A–H, next to each day. You will hear the conversation twice.

[pause]

Man:	Hello, Diana. I've just got this information about some new evening courses. On Monday evenings, they've got some guitar classes.
Diana:	I'm busy on Mondays. What can you do on Tuesdays?
Man:	Well, there's a course to teach you how to make easy meals from different parts of the world. The teacher's Terry Wood. He's in the restaurant business.
Diana:	That sounds good. What about Wednesdays?
Man:	That class is about the cinema in Italy and France.
Diana:	Oh, I'd like that. Is there a course for you – something on business perhaps?
Man:	Well, on Thursdays, there's one looking at different companies around the world. If you do it, you spend a lot of time on the college computers, which is good.
Diana:	Oh.
Man:	There's another interesting course on Friday. You learn about the moon and all the different stars.
Diana:	Really? Is there anything on Saturday?
Man:	Yes, then you can learn about the lives and work of the world's greatest painters.
Diana:	I think the Wednesday course sounds best.

[pause]

Now listen again.

[repeat]

[pause]

That is the end of Part Two.

[pause]

PART 3   *Now look at Part Three.*

[pause]

Listen to a girl asking for information about a coach trip to Edinburgh. For questions 11–15, tick A, B or C. You will hear the conversation twice. Look at questions 11–15 now. You have 20 seconds.

[pause]

Now listen to the conversation.

Girl:	Good morning. Can I book a coach trip to Edinburgh?
Man:	Yes, there are two every day, morning and afternoon.
Girl:	Tomorrow morning, please. It's my free day. How much is it?
Man:	It's nine pounds for adults, five for children, and seven for students.
Girl:	That's good. I'm at the university. Here's the money and my student card.
Man:	Thanks. Here's your ticket.
Girl:	Where can I catch the coach?
Man:	In Bridge Street or outside the Grand Hotel, or there's a stop at the library if you want to wait there.
Girl:	Good idea, I'll do that. What time does it leave?

Man:	It leaves Bridge Street at quarter to nine and gets to you at five to nine. It takes ten minutes going through town.
Girl:	Is there time to see the castle in Edinburgh?
Man:	Yes, we go there after the cathedral. We don't visit the shops or museums, I'm afraid.
Girl:	Fine. How long is the trip?
Man:	The journey there and back is about two and a quarter hours and you spend two hours in Edinburgh. So that's four hours and fifteen minutes. You'll be back by lunchtime.
Girl:	Great!

[pause]

Now listen again.

[repeat]

[pause]

That is the end of Part Three.

[pause]

PART 4   *Now look at Part Four.*

[pause]

You will hear the manager of a shop leaving a message for a customer. Listen and complete questions 16–20. You will hear the conversation twice.

[pause]

Bob Watson:	Hello, can I speak to Anna Jones, please?
Mrs Jones:	I'm afraid she's out but you can leave a message with me – I'm her mother.
Bob Watson:	Thanks. This is Bob Watson from the shoe shop Forsters.
Mrs Jones:	How do you spell that?
Bob Watson:	It's F O R S T E R S.
Mrs Jones:	OK, I've got that.
Bob Watson:	Can you tell her that we now have the boots she wanted in size thirty-eight? We only had size forty when she came into the shop last week. And she'll be pleased to know that they're also in the colour she liked – green. Before we only had black ones.
Mrs Jones:	That's good news.
Bob Watson:	Yes, and there's even more good news. We're having a sale, so they're forty pounds cheaper. Now they're sixty-five pounds, which is a good price. They're made of very good leather.
Mrs Jones:	Well, she'll be really pleased. Can she come and get them tomorrow at around five o'clock?
Bob Watson:	She'll have to come before two o'clock, I'm afraid, because that's when we shut tomorrow.
Mrs Jones:	OK, I'll tell her.

[pause]

Now listen again.

[repeat]

[pause]

That is the end of Part Four.

[pause]

PART 5   *Now look at Part Five.*

[pause]

You will hear a man on the radio giving information about an art class. Listen and complete questions 21–25. You will hear the information twice.

[pause]

Next week is Family Learning Week and there will be special activities at colleges and schools all over town.

There is a very interesting art class at Hadley College called 'Paint with your Parents'. It's on Saturday, October the ninth, and is for anyone with children under the age of sixteen. It's a two-hour class. It begins at ten fifteen in the morning and finishes at twelve fifteen.

The most interesting thing about this class is the special guest, a famous writer called J.P. Hayward – that's H A Y W A R D. She will read from her latest book, *Dark Lake*. Listening to her will give you ideas to use in your paintings.

The class is not expensive. A family ticket costs eight pounds seventy. That's for four people. Anyone extra has to pay three pounds.

This class will be very popular, so book early. The number you need to call is double four nine seven, six three nine oh. I hope you all enjoy Family Learning Week.

[pause]

Now listen again.

[repeat]

[pause]

That is the end of Part Five.

You now have eight minutes to write your answers on the answer sheet.

Note: Teacher, stop the recording here and time eight minutes. Remind the students when there is **one** minute remaining.

[pause]

That is the end of the test.

Test 4 Answer key

Paper 1   Reading and Writing

Part 1
1 G   **2** F   **3** D   **4** A   **5** H

Part 2
6 C   **7** B   **8** C   **9** A   **10** A

Part 3
11 A   **12** C   **13** A   **14** B   **15** B   **16** H   **17** D   **18** A   **19** F   **20** B

Part 4
21 B   **22** C   **23** B   **24** A   **25** B   **26** C   **27** A

Part 5
28 B   **29** B   **30** A   **31** C   **32** A   **33** C   **34** B   **35** A

Part 6
For questions 36–40, spelling must be correct.
36 menu   **37** dictionary   **38** journalist   **39** library   **40** glasses

Part 7
For questions 41–50, ignore capitals / absence of capitals. Spelling must be correct.
41 to/into   **42** not   **43** lot/few/number/group/grp   **44** by   **45** than   **46** it/that/this
47 the   **48** see/hear   **49** If/When/Should/As/Since/Provided   **50** be/feel

Part 8
For questions 51–55, spelling must be correct.
51 Spanish   **52** Wed(nesday)(s)   **53** 15(th) December   **54** 14(weeks)   **55** (£)105(.00)

Part 9
Question 56
The three parts of the message that must be communicated are:

i   where your music club is
ii   the day the club meets
iii   details of what you do at the club.

Sample answer A

Mark: 3

> Dear Jools
> Hi. first I want tell you, the address of muisc club
> The music club is only open on Fridays.
> There, you can play every thing do you want!
> Thanks
> Naveed

Two parts of the message are clearly communicated but one part (i) is unattempted.

Sample answer B

Mark: 0

> My dear, Jools
> I got your email yestarday I am very happy which club you going the music
> I would like be an some westean music and pope music I think that sort is
> god for me
> yours faithful Stefano

The question has not been attempted (the response does not relate to the prompts).

Sample answer C

Mark: 2

> Dear Jools
> How are you to day?
> I will go to the start music
> I will go that at the weekend and I will dance and liste some music.
> see you soon

There is some relevant content to two points (ii and iii) but the response is unclear.

Sample answer D

Mark: 4

> Jools,
> I go to music club every Saturday night's in college. It has got a lot of musical enstrumant than I'll learn to playing piano there. Do you want to learn playing musical enstrumant you can come, on Saturday night's in college
> Love Esen

All three parts of the message are communicated, but with some awkwardness of expression.

Sample answer E

Mark: 5

> Dear Jools,
> thanks for your email. I go every Monday to the music club on the High Street. I'm studying to play the piano. Come to hear me,
> with love Maria

All three parts of the message are clearly communicated.

Paper 2   Listening

Part 1

1 A   **2** B   **3** B   **4** C   **5** B

Part 2

6 G   **7** E   **8** B   **9** F   **10** A

Part 3

11 C   **12** C   **13** B   **14** A   **15** A

Part 4

16 bridge   **17** 12.15 / twelve fifteen / (a) quarter past twelve (pm)
18 ALDFORD   **19** (drinks and) ice(-)cream(s)
20 (£)3.95 / three (pounds) (and) ninety(-)five (p/pence)

Part 5

21 (£)89(.00) / eighty(-)nine (pound(s))   **22** lunch(es)
23 Fri(day)/week   **24** July   **25** 8447 6953

Ben: Well, it *is* a business trip – and the weather will be different everywhere I go.

Ben's wife: I suppose on Sunday you'll travel in your jeans.

Ben: Yes. Then on Monday I'm going to meet the company boss, so I'll need my suit then. I can't wear jeans.

Ben's wife: What's happening on Tuesday?

Ben: I'm visiting a factory in the south, so I've packed these grey trousers. They're light and I won't need a jacket – it'll be thirty-five degrees!

Ben's wife: Oh! Then you're in the mountains on Wednesday.

Ben: Yes. A jacket won't be warm enough. I've got my coat for that day.

Ben's wife: Are you taking a sweater as well?

Ben: There isn't room in the suitcase. On Thursday I'll be by the sea, so I'm taking my swimming shorts.

Ben's wife: And what about Friday?

Ben: I'm having lunch with some colleagues. I'll wear that blue shirt you gave me. Look, here it is, under the suit.

Ben's wife: Oh good.

[pause]

Now listen again.

[repeat]

[pause]

That is the end of Part Two.

[pause]

PART 3   *Now look at Part Three.*

[pause]

Listen to Duncan talking to a friend about a tennis course. For questions 11–15, tick A, B or C. You will hear the conversation twice. Look at questions 11–15 now. You have 20 seconds.

[pause]

Now listen to the conversation.

Girl: Hi Duncan. How was your tennis course at the weekend?

Duncan: Well, I was actually there for five days, not two.

Girl: Oh! Was the hotel nice?

Duncan: Beautiful! We were high up in the mountains. We looked down on the lake, where we swam every morning, and across to the town on the other side.

Girl: Was the teacher good?

Duncan: Excellent. He's worked here in England for ages but he was born in Canada, so he speaks French and English.

Girl: I'd like to do the course. Was it very expensive?

Duncan: Um, the full price in the summer is two hundred and sixty-five pounds, but it only cost me two hundred and five pounds because I'm a student. In the autumn it's less – a hundred and eighty-five pounds.

Girl: Hmm. Did you have to buy anything special?

Duncan: I already had tennis clothes, and the hotel had racquets and balls, but I got some new shoes because my old tennis ones were too small.

Girl: What did you do in the evenings?

Duncan: Sometimes we watched videos of tennis matches, but on the last night we danced and sang songs in the hotel garden. That was great!

[pause]

Now listen again.

[repeat]

[pause]

That is the end of Part Three.

[pause]

PART 4 *Now look at Part Four.*

[pause]

You will hear a woman phoning for information about a boat trip. Listen and complete questions 16–20. You will hear the conversation twice.

[pause]

Man: Hello. Tourist Information.

Woman: Hello, I'm phoning about the boat trips on the River Dee. Can you tell me which days they are?

Man: Every Friday and Sunday.

Woman: And where does the boat leave from?

Man: You'll find it next to the bridge. It's ten minutes' walk from North Street car park.

Woman: Are there several trips a day?

Man: Just one. It starts at twelve fifteen. It takes about an hour and forty-five minutes, so you'll be back by two.

Woman: How far up the river will the boat take us?

Man: All the way to Aldford. That's A L D F O R D. You get off there and come back through the mountains on a bus.

Woman: It sounds nice. Can I get any food on the boat?

Man: Not much. They only sell ice cream and cold drinks. But there are lots of cafés in Aldford.

Woman: Can we get tickets on the boat?

Man: Yes. They're three pounds ninety-five for adults and two pounds seventy-five for children. Come early and get a good seat.

Woman: OK. Thank you for your help.

[pause]

Now listen again.

[repeat]

[pause]

That is the end of Part Four.

[pause]

PART 5   *Now look at Part Five.*

[pause]

You will hear a woman giving information on the radio about a theatre school. Listen and complete questions 21–25. You will hear the information twice.

[pause]

Do you love singing, dancing and acting? Then come to Silver Star Theatre School. We have courses every week during the school holidays for children between nine and sixteen years old.

If you are fourteen, fifteen or sixteen, the price is only eighty-nine pounds for a week. If you are under fourteen, it costs ninety-five pounds per week. You'll find we are cheaper than other theatre schools but much better!

The only thing you should bring with you is your lunch. We will give you any special clothes you need.

From Monday to Thursday you will work really hard. Then family and friends can come and watch you in a special show on Friday afternoon. For many people, this is the best day of the week.

The first summer course begins on July the twenty-first and you must book by the twelfth. If you want to join the Silver Star school, call Mary and ask for a booking form today. The phone number is eight double four seven, six nine five three, and you can call between nine a.m. and five p.m. every day.

[pause]

Now listen again.

[repeat]

[pause]

That is the end of Part Five.

You now have eight minutes to write your answers on the answer sheet.

Note: Teacher, stop the recording here and time eight minutes. Remind the students when there is **one** minute remaining.

[pause]

That is the end of the test.

Sample answer sheet – Reading and Writing (Sheet 1)

UNIVERSITY *of* CAMBRIDGE
ESOL Examinations

SAMPLE

Candidate Name
If not already printed, write name
in CAPITALS and complete the
Candidate No. grid (in pencil).

Candidate Signature

Examination Title

Centre

Supervisor:
If the candidate is ABSENT or has WITHDRAWN shade here

Centre No.

Candidate No.

Examination
Details

KET Paper 1 Reading and Writing Candidate Answer Sheet

Instructions

Use a PENCIL (B or HB).
Rub out any answer you want to change with an eraser.

For Parts 1, 2, 3, 4 and 5:
Mark ONE letter for each question.
For example, if you think C is the right answer to the
question, mark your answer sheet like this:

0 A B C

Part 1

1	A B C D E F G H
2	A B C D E F G H
3	A B C D E F G H
4	A B C D E F G H
5	A B C D E F G H

Part 2

6	A B C
7	A B C
8	A B C
9	A B C
10	A B C

Part 3

11	A B C	16	A B C D E F G H
12	A B C	17	A B C D E F G H
13	A B C	18	A B C D E F G H
14	A B C	19	A B C D E F G H
15	A B C	20	A B C D E F G H

Part 4

21	A B C
22	A B C
23	A B C
24	A B C
25	A B C
26	A B C
27	A B C

Part 5

28	A B C
29	A B C
30	A B C
31	A B C
32	A B C
33	A B C
34	A B C
35	A B C

Turn over for
Parts 6 - 9 →

Sample answer sheet – Reading and Writing (Sheet 2)

For **Parts 6, 7 and 8:**

Write your answers in the spaces next to the numbers (36 to 55) like this:

0	example

Part 6		Do not write here
36		1 36 0
37		1 37 0
38		1 38 0
39		1 39 0
40		1 40 0

Part 7		Do not write here
41		1 41 0
42		1 42 0
43		1 43 0
44		1 44 0
45		1 45 0
46		1 46 0
47		1 47 0
48		1 48 0
49		1 49 0
50		1 50 0

Part 8		Do not write here
51		1 51 0
52		1 52 0
53		1 53 0
54		1 54 0
55		1 55 0

Part 9 (Question 56): Write your answer below.

Do not write below (Examiner use only)
0   1   2   3   4   5

Sample answer sheet – Listening

UNIVERSITY *of* CAMBRIDGE
ESOL Examinations

S A M P L E

Candidate Name
If not already printed, write name
in CAPITALS and complete the
Candidate No. grid (in pencil).

Candidate Signature

Examination Title

Centre

Supervisor:

If the candidate is ABSENT or has WITHDRAWN shade here ▭

Centre No.

Candidate No.

Examination
Details

0	0	0	0
1	1	1	1
2	2	2	2
3	3	3	3
4	4	4	4
5	5	5	5
6	6	6	6
7	7	7	7
8	8	8	8
9	9	9	9

KET Paper 2 Listening Candidate Answer Sheet

Instructions

Use a PENCIL (B or HB).

Rub out any answer you want to change with an eraser.

For **Parts 1, 2** and **3**:
Mark ONE letter for each question.
For example, if you think **C** is the right answer to the
question, mark your answer sheet like this:

0 A B C̶

Part 1		Part 2		Part 3	
1	A B C	6	A B C D E F G H	11	A B C
2	A B C	7	A B C D E F G H	12	A B C
3	A B C	8	A B C D E F G H	13	A B C
4	A B C	9	A B C D E F G H	14	A B C
5	A B C	10	A B C D E F G H	15	A B C

For **Parts 4** and **5**:
Write your answers in the spaces next to the
numbers (16 to 25) like this:

0 example

Part 4		Do not write here	Part 5		Do not write here
16		1 16 0	21		1 21 0
17		1 17 0	22		1 22 0
18		1 18 0	23		1 23 0
19		1 19 0	24		1 24 0
20		1 20 0	25		1 25 0